BISEXUAL MEN EXIST

of related interest

Bi the Way
The Bisexual Guide to Life
Lois Shearing
ISBN 978 1 78775 290 0
eISBN 978 1 78775 291 7

Coming Out Stories
Personal Experiences of Coming Out from Across the LGBTQ+ Spectrum
Edited by Emma Goswell and Sam Walker
Foreword by Tim Sigsworth MBE
ISBN 978 1 78775 495 9
eISBN 978 1 78775 496 6

Queer Body Power
Finding Your Body Positivity
Essie Dennis
ISBN 978 1 78775 904 6
eISBN 978 1 78775 905 3

LGBTQIA+ Pride Sticker Book
Jessica Kingsley Publishers
ISBN 978 1 83997 246 1
Illustrated by Ollie Mann

Bisexual Men Exist

A Handbook for Bisexual, Pansexual and
M-Spec Men

Vaneet Mehta

Jessica Kingsley Publishers
London and Philadelphia

First published in Great Britain in 2023 by Jessica Kingsley Publishers
An imprint of Hodder & Stoughton Ltd
An Hachette Company

1

The information contained in this book is not intended to replace the services of trained medical professionals or to be a substitute for medical advice. You are advised to consult a doctor on any matters relating to your health, and in particular on any matters that may require diagnosis or medical attention.

A CIP catalogue record for this title is available from the British Library and the Library of Congress

ISBN 978 1 78775 719 6
eISBN 978 1 78775 720 2

Printed and bound in Great Britain by Clays Ltd

Jessica Kingsley Publishers' policy is to use papers that are natural, renewable and recyclable products and made from wood grown in sustainable forests. The logging and manufacturing processes are expected to conform to the environmental regulations of the country of origin.

Jessica Kingsley Publishers
Carmelite House
50 Victoria Embankment
London EC4Y 0DZ

www.jkp.com

To Mrs Stevens for believing in me when I did not.

To Joseph for inspiring me.

To Chay for uplifting me.

To Lauren and Ellen for giving me a voice.

Without you, I would not be where I am today.

Contents

Introduction

Being an m-spec man is no easy task. I should know. I spent over a decade grappling with my sexuality, finding ways to deny it or push it aside, before I eventually came out. Then I was met with a minefield of being questioned, erased, ridiculed and rejected from numerous different angles, which didn't go away when I entered LGBTQIA + (lesbian, gay, bisexual, transgender, queer or questioning, intersex, asexual, aromantic or agender and others) spaces. I have struggled, and at times still struggle, with recognizing and embracing my identity, every part of it.

I felt I went years being uninformed and ignorant about m-spec identities, which only became deeper and deeper ingrained and internalized. I had to spend so much time and energy to unwork this in my head in order to accept myself. This struggle was made so much harder due to the invisibility of m-spec men.

This was part of the reason why I created my hashtag, #BisexualMenExist. Partly it was to help combat the hate and erasure that m-spec men receive, to drown it out with a positive message.

Partly it was to help educate people, to make the masses realize that we are here and there are a significant number of us. Partly it was to help me connect with more people like myself, to find my people, my queer m-spec brothers and siblings.

But the main reason was to help those who were like me, who felt so alone and trapped and who struggled to accept their identity. I wanted to help those who were questioning, those who were in denial and closeted, all those m-spec men hiding away, to embrace themselves and be who they truly are by realizing that they aren't alone in their fight.

This book is truly an extension of that. In this book, I navigate through a number of key areas of m-spec men's lives, from coming out to dating, relationships and health. I discuss the importance of representation and education and how that underpins the issues we experience, look through the lens of various intersectional identities and explore the treatment of m-spec men in LGBTQIA + spaces. I unpack the issues that m-spec men experience and bring in people's personal experiences to highlight the impact these issues have on real people, including myself. I mainly focus on the UK and US through the statistics I use, and while the contributors come from all over, the vast majority are from the UK and US.

What is m-spec?

Before I get into these various topics, I should first cover the basics. First, what is m-spec? M-spec stands for multi-gender attracted spectrum, so it covers all of the various identities where their attraction is not limited to a single gender. Some labels that come under this umbrella are bisexual, pansexual, polysexual, omnisexual and many more. These labels all have their own definition, their own flag and their own community. Here are some definitions of the four I have mentioned above:

- bisexual – attraction to more than one gender
- pansexual – attraction regardless of gender
- polysexual – attraction to multiple genders
- omnisexual – attraction to all genders.

However, these labels also have a broad overlap, as you may see from the definitions. The way people identify may place them in one, two, or even all of these labels. But identity is a very personal thing, and the labels that people choose to use are up to them and what they personally feel comfortable with.

People may choose to only use one label exclusively, or use numerous labels interchangeably. Someone may align closely with one definition but personally choose to use another. And the reasons for doing so can range wildly, from the label being more well known to liking the colour of the flag better.

This is important to remember. At the end of the day, it is us who make the label have meaning, not the other way around. And all the labels are valid. They don't take away from each other and no one should be forced to use one over the other, for any reason.

As mentioned, all of these labels have a lot in common. They all identify people as multi-gender attracted, m-spec. Some people use bisexual+, bisexual or bi as an umbrella term instead; however, not all m-spec people like this. This is because it can erase the individuality of these labels, painting them all as 'basically bi' and ignoring the key differences between the terms.

While my hashtag focused on bisexual men, I did invite

other m-spec people to join in. Some did, but not everyone was comfortable with that. Some changed it up, switching bisexual to pansexual for example, which I completely welcomed.

I am not immune to treating bi as an umbrella term; in fact the title of this book does the same. The issues I discuss in this book aren't exclusive to bisexual men, but affect all m-spec men. While the majority of people involved in this book may be bisexual, not everyone uses this term or uses it exclusively.

So throughout this book, I have opted to use the term m-spec. This is to acknowledge that these issues aren't exclusive to bisexual men and bisexual is not a suitable umbrella for all m-spec men. I use this wherever possible, but when referencing texts I revert to the terminology they use within their text.

Who are the contributors?

While this book may have 'men' in the title, not everyone included in the book necessarily identifies as a man. Some may use man in conjunction with other labels, while others may not use man at all. Non-binary, genderqueer and genderfluid are just some of the labels some of the contributors use. I do not wish to erase these people's identities through the process of this book, so I thought it important to bring attention to this fact here.

These people, with the title of this book in mind, have been willing to share their story with me as they believe it has relevance to the topic at hand. This may be due to how they previously identified themselves as a man or how society perceives them, potentially due to the way in which they present.

What this highlights is the binary view in which society perceives people's gender, labelling people as either a man or a woman and erasing their actual gender identity. Some may experience misogyny based on their gender presentation, while others may experience misandry. What this means is that some of the experiences that these people have may be similar to those of m-spec men. Throughout this book, I will be referring to m-spec men and the way in which the structures in society create certain barriers and bigotry that impact them specifically. But it is important to note that this particular breed of m-spec phobia and erasure is not faced by m-spec men alone.

CHAPTER 1

Representation and Education

Representation and education play a big role in our society. Education allows people to understand the complexities of the world around them and grasp the differences we see in society. It can help people gain acceptance of those who are different from them and understand their struggles.

Education is often understood as attending school; however, traditional schooling has not always provided the right information or support for those within the LGBTQIA + community. This may be due to laws, an outdated curriculum, unequipped staff or even personal bigotry among faculty.

But there are other sources of education besides traditional schooling, such as various forms of media. Representation, whether that be on TV, in films or written in books, can help educate people about the variety in society. This can be fictional stories with characters from different walks of life, or non-fictional representation from pop idols to Hollywood celebrities.

Not only that, but representation can help people see themselves reflected in society. It can help people see their own story as valid and make them feel less alone in the world. It can help them own themselves and put into words their experiences and hardship. This is incredibly important for LGBTQIA + people, to know that there are other people who identify as they do and that there is a community out there.

According to GLAAD's *Where We Are On TV* report for 2019–2020, 26 per cent of LGBTQ characters are bisexual+ despite some studies showing that bisexual people make up the majority (52%) of LGB people (Movement Advancement Project 2016). The majority of bisexual+ characters shown on screen are women, at 70 per cent, while only 28 per cent are men and 2 per cent are non-binary.

In real terms, this gives us 36 bisexual+ men on screen during 2019–2020, which is a pretty decent number. However, this is the representation we see on screen in the present day. If we go back just a few years and look at GLAAD's *Where We Are On TV* report from 2014–2015, there were only two bisexual+ men. This clearly shows that there was a lack of historic m-spec representation on TV, which would likely have had an impact on m-spec men on their journey of self-discovery.

Having education and representation is just one side of the coin. Simply having it is not enough. How are m-spec identities portrayed in media? What are people taught about m-spec people? Is the representation or education actually helping the community, or causing more harm?

In this chapter, I will be going through some examples showing the m-spec erasure and phobia that is within the representation we see. I will be discussing how this poor representation, as well as education, only causes further harm to m-spec men.

Lack of representation

I personally had an idea that I was 'not straight' when I was around ten. I say 'not straight' as I had no idea what my sexuality was. I found myself having crushes on the girls in my class, but also being weirdly intrigued by the boys as well. The only labels I was aware of were straight and gay, and I couldn't explain my feelings into either one of these categories. Bisexual and m-spec identities were something I was completely unaware of – the label had simply not entered my vocabulary.

The lack of representation played a big part here. The GLAAD *Where We Are On TV* reports give us a great insight into the LGBTQ representation we see on screen. From 2010 to today, it can be seen that the representation of bisexual+ men has been increasing over the years, but the historic lack of representation will naturally have had an impact on m-spec men.

I was ten in 2002 and unfortunately I cannot find a report from that far back. But when looking at the 2009–2010 report – the earliest one I can find – it shows that out of the 16 LGB characters on screen there were only four bisexual women and no bisexual men as regular characters on broadcast networks. I don't think it's a stretch to assume that the representation on screen from 2002 would not have been better.

At the age of ten and throughout my teens, I can recall several gay and lesbian characters, but no m-spec characters whatsoever. Shows which included representation of gay or lesbian characters often portrayed sexuality as a binary concept, straight or gay. Any characters who showed indications of being attracted to more than one gender were either left ambiguous or forced into either straight or gay.

'No bisexuals' trope

There are several TV tropes of note here. One trope is 'no bisexuals' (TV Tropes, No Bisexuals), which is when the fictional world for the piece of media simply does not include bisexual or m-spec people whatsoever. This often leads to storylines where a character will change from straight to gay, and in some cases even the reverse will happen.

A notable example of this for me is *Buffy the Vampire Slayer*. In seasons 1 to 3, Willow is shown to be straight. She shows attraction to multiple men and has a long-standing relationship with the character Oz, as well as a fling with Xander. However, this changes in season 4.

In season 4, we are introduced to a new character, Tara. Willow starts having feelings for Tara and this causes her to question her sexuality. It is presented somewhat ambiguously at first, not clearly defining the relationship they have nor the fact that Willow is a lesbian. Willow still shows lingering feelings for Oz when he returns to visit her. But after this, these feelings seem to disappear entirely and the show starts doubling down on her new-found sexuality. There are several storylines where the show makes it abundantly clear that she is into women, and only women. In the season 7 episode 'Him', a spell causes Willow (along with other women) to fall for a man. The other characters try to snap her out of it, reminding her that she's gay.

Now this may be an entirely valid experience for some lesbian and gay people. Not everyone knows their sexuality from a young age and may find themselves in different sex relationships, only to explore their sexuality as they get older and realize that they're actually gay/lesbian. New experiences can bring about new understanding of your identity. I don't wish to discredit that. However, this also felt like a missed opportunity.

With Willow's history with men whom she was clearly deeply in love with, and no indication of any doubt during these relationships, her new-found attraction to Tara could have been a breakthrough for her realizing she was m-spec.

But unfortunately, this isn't what occurred. It felt like m-spec erasure was being played out on screen, which was incredibly invalidating.

This issue was addressed by Joss Whedon himself, the creator and executive producer of *Buffy*. He stated in an interview with *Metro* that he was pressured into making Willow not bisexual (Griffiths 2020). There were fears that it would make same-sex attraction appear as a phase and cause harm to lesbian people, which misses the fact that this binary approach to sexuality caused harm to bisexual and m-spec people.

A similar storyline occurred in 2008's *90210*, this time with a man. The character of Teddy first enters the show in season 2 and, as with all men on these teen dramas, is portrayed as a ladies' man, a player. He briefly dates Adrianna before getting into a long-term relationship with Silver, two women who made the main cast of the show. However, this changed in season 3.

After getting drunk at a party, Teddy ends up sleeping with another man called Ian. Teddy starts going through the motions of coming out. He starts with denying it and trying to reaffirm his straight identity, which doesn't work out. He slowly starts exploring his sexuality by visiting gay bars and starts a secret relationship with Ian. Eventually, he comes out to his friends as gay.

Yet again, this feels like a missed opportunity. His history with women was always shown authentically, that he was truly in love with them. In order to explain this the show had Teddy and Silver talk about their history and confirmed that, while he did indeed love her, he was lying to himself throughout their relationship.

Again, I do not wish to take away from the experiences of gay or lesbian people. This may be entirely valid and what many people go through. But the experiences of m-spec people are equally as valid, but were never shown. The above are simply two examples in a sea of many similar storylines, having characters go from straight to gay without any consideration of other identities, not even so much as a mention.

'Ambiguously bi' trope

Another trope is the 'ambiguously bi' trope (TV Tropes, Ambiguously Bi). Now what makes a character ambiguously bisexual or m-spec is, naturally, ambiguous. For some, the representation may have been clear, for others not so much. Often, m-spec representation isn't labelled as such. Of course, this is a valid choice – plenty of people choose not to label their orientation – but when done in media it creates room for debate. Characters may be shown to be attracted to people of multiple genders, but it often won't be simultaneously. This raises the question of whether the character is in fact m-spec, or if they now identify as gay like countless other characters before them.

In order to examine the quality of m-spec representation, Shearing created the Ramirez Test, named after the actor Sara Ramirez (Shearing 2019). It poses three questions:

1. Is the character recognizable as bisexual within the media itself?

2. Is the character's bisexuality presented as a joke or flaw?

3. Does the character ever say that they're bi/pansexual? (Shearing 2019)

So while some character's multi-gendered attraction may appear apparent in the media, and be presented well, it is often lacking the third and final step, the gold standard of representation. The debate over the character's identity can leave m-spec people out in the cold.

An example is Eleanor from *The Good Place*. Can we really say that she provides m-spec representation? She shows attraction to Tahani, and in one of the 'reboots' is partnered up with her, but we never see their relationship. We don't see her express attraction for any other women and we don't see any former relationships that aren't with a man. Of course, none of this means that she can't be m-spec; this is all entirely valid. But that, coupled with the fact that she doesn't state her sexuality outright, means people may read her attraction to Tahani in different ways. This ambiguity creates debate, which often leads to erasure.

Impact of lack of representation

This lack of representation was felt from all the m-spec men I spoke to for this book. Not a single person could give me an example of an m-spec character they saw in media when they started experiencing attraction to more than one gender. This lack of representation created a complete lack of awareness of m-spec identities, such as bisexual. Many of the men I spoke to told me that while they were aware of gay and straight, bisexual or pansexual had never entered their vocabulary.

Think about the impact m-spec representation could have had here, how it could have opened the door to understanding sexuality as more complex than the binary notion that is fed to us. Think about how it could have broadened our horizons and given us the language to explain our feelings.

I started watching *Buffy* around the time I had these confusing feelings. This was, to my knowledge, my first encounter with the binary construct of sexuality being reinforced. I was aware of both gay and straight, but to see someone like Willow move from one to the other limited my understanding of sexuality. It boxed it in. I saw this and it became clear to me that there were only two options.

I think about how different things could have been if Willow had come out as bisexual instead. It could have been a lightbulb moment for me, but instead it forced me to pick a side and deepened my denial.

Kamal told me how he found this character development frustrating. He felt that if they had explored the idea of her being a lesbian prior, showing how she felt pressured into compulsory heterosexuality, it would have worked better and made her desires clear. Instead, they moved away from the possibility of bisexuality.

I didn't learn about the term bisexual until I was around 17. In fact, the word I heard first was bicurious, due to someone in my school choosing to come out as such. While I had now learned the word, the binary idea of sexuality had become so deeply ingrained that I couldn't accept bisexuality as valid and, therefore, was unable to relate my feelings to it.

As I saw the same storyline play out again and again, the validity of m-spec identities became more and more far-fetched. Teddy's storyline in 90210 occurred after I'd learned the word bisexual. I still recall watching the episode where he slept with a man and wondering if this meant he was m-spec. I watched this episode with a housemate while I was at university, who immediately exclaimed that he was gay on watching this scene.

I rocked the boat at this point, decided to test the waters, and questioned whether he was gay, suggesting that he could be bisexual instead. My housemate rejected this idea, stating unequivocally that sleeping with a man meant that he was gay. Yet again, this reinforced the idea that sexuality was a binary concept.

Real-life representation

This issue is not just within the fictional world of film and TV, but with pop culture figures too. Freddie Mercury, the lead singer of Queen, was one such person who was seen as gay despite there being ample evidence that he was bisexual. Freddie was known to have romantic and sexual relationships with people of all genders. He came out as bisexual to his partner Mary Austin, which is public knowledge (Wright 2019).

However, bisexuality and m-spec identities in the 1980s were even less well known than they are now and were erased pretty readily. Many community spaces were labelled 'lesbian and gay' and these were used as umbrella terms, which often led to erasure of bisexual and m-spec people in these spaces. Todd, a bisexual man who grew up in the 1980s, was impacted by this m-spec erasure and blames the media for it, saying that bisexual is often harder to explain than gay.

Even to this day, many see Freddie Mercury as someone who went from straight to gay. Again, we see that same binary view of sexuality played out even on real people. Freddie Mercury wasn't alone in this. David Bowie can be seen in interviews from around the same time, being quizzed on his sexuality, with the interviewer clearly not accepting bisexual as a final answer (Thames TV 2016). There is a complete refusal to accept m-spec men for their identity.

Lack of education

Of course, representation is only part of the story here; the other side of this is education. Both representation and education go hand in hand and can help people understand their sexuality, feel secure in its validity and comfortable identifying as LGBTQIA+. But education on LGBTQIA + identities within schools was not something that historically happened.

In the UK, Section 28 (of the Local Government Act) meant that LGBTQIA+ education was not allowed to be taught in school in England, Scotland and Wales (LGBT History Month, n.d.). The law stated that a local authority 'shall not intentionally promote homosexuality' or 'promote the teaching in any maintained school of the acceptability of homosexuality as a pretended family relationship' (LGBT History Month, n.d.).

This was repealed in Scotland in 2000 and in England and Wales in 2003. This meant as I was growing up in England, my school did not provide any form of LGBTQIA+ education. While this act was repealed as I entered secondary school, the curriculum was not updated accordingly to make education more inclusive. This meant that even though schools were permitted to teach LGBTQIA+ information, it was still missing and I, as well as others, went through school without LGBTQIA+ education.

In fact, according to Stonewall's *School Report* published in 2017, 40 per cent of LGBT students are never taught about LGBT issues, only 20 per cent of them learned about safe sex in same-sex relationships and, most importantly, 76 per cent of them never learned about bisexuality (Stonewall 2017). It is evident that even as recently as 2017, there was still a large gap in education around LGBTQIA+ identities, especially m-spec identities.

The US has issues when it comes to LGBTQIA+ inclusive

education as well. One survey from 2015 shows that only 12 per cent of those surveyed say that same-sex relationships were covered in their sex education class (Public Religion Research Institute 2015). According to Planned Parenthood (Planned Parenthood 2015), only 19 per cent of secondary schools in the US had LGBTQ inclusive sex education. As of 2020, there was no countrywide programme mandating LGBTQ inclusive sex education (Kuhr 2020). According to the Sexuality Information and Education Council of the United States (SIECUS) in 2020, only 11 states had policies to include positive LGBTQ education and discussion (SIECUS 2020).

Of course, this impacts all LGBTQIA+ people, not just m-spec people. But naturally those identities that have permeated less through society, such as m-spec identities along with others outside gay and lesbian, suffer a far greater impact, both historically and to this day.

Negative representation

The other major issue is negative representation and education. Having representation in and of itself isn't useful if it misrepresents m-spec identities and falls into harmful tropes. This only serves to build a bad image around m-spec identities and discourages people to use such labels for their identity. Again, there are tropes that come into play here.

'Just an experiment' trope

One of these tropes is the 'just an experiment' trope (LGBT Fans Deserve Better, n.d.). This is when a character displays attraction that would appear to be m-spec, only for the character to move on from it and re-identify as straight or gay.

Back to 2008's 90210: the character Adrianna only shows attraction to men until season 2, when she becomes attracted to a woman, Gia, and enters a relationship with her. At this point, she appears to be m-spec, but ambiguously as this is never stated outright, and just assumed due to her history. After Adrianna and Gia break up, this relationship is filed away as a phase. From recollection, there is even an episode where Adrianna recommends to all of her friends to try it.

Again, this is likely to be an experience some can relate to, as many people may have had moments in their life where they've experimented with their sexuality, especially in their youth. But when m-spec identities are constantly displayed in such a way it can be harmful, particularly when there is no long-standing m-spec representation within that media. It makes these identities as a whole appear to be a phase, a moment everyone has throughout their life, and eventually people will move on from it into either straight or gay.

Another example of this is Blaine from *Glee*. In season 2, episode 14, 'Blame It On The Alcohol', the characters have a party, get drunk and decide to play spin the bottle. When Rachel spins the bottle, it lands on Blaine. Blaine, who identifies as gay, shares a drunken kiss with Rachel. Later, he reveals to Kurt, who also identifies as gay and holds feelings for Blaine, that he enjoyed the kiss with Rachel, and accepts Rachel's request for a date. This ignites a torrent of abuse from Kurt, which is only inflamed further when Blaine mentions that he could be bisexual.

Kurt hurls a number of m-spec phobic comments both at Blaine and throughout the episode to various other characters, including his dad and Rachel. In order to confirm where Blaine lies, Rachel decides to kiss Blaine when they are both sober.

This causes Blaine to reveal that he is '100 per cent gay' and the confusion around his sexuality is cleared up entirely.

This has a number of distressing connotations. As Kurt spews his m-spec phobia throughout the episode, he is never fully challenged, nor properly educated. He doesn't change his opinion or show any signs of learning, nor does he apologize for his comments to Blaine or others. When Blaine reveals that he is in fact gay, it almost vindicates Kurt and justifies his comments since his adamance that Blaine is gay is in fact correct.

The conclusion from this is that Blaine's bisexuality was nothing more than a drunken moment, and that bisexual feelings can be dismissed under alcohol use. The idea that Blaine's confusion can be 'cleared up' with a simple sober kiss with a girl is simplifying sexuality and sexual experiences. He could easily be bisexual and just not into Rachel, but this isn't explored. The idea that bisexuality is nothing more than a tool for gay men to 'feel normal' or closet themselves is never once challenged and is only reinforced by this ending.

The fact that this m-spec phobia was said by a gay man, and the show itself is created and produced by a gay man, only makes the situation more painful. It shows the issues that m-spec people have to go through, even within the LGBTQIA+ community, and how gay men see m-spec men as closeted, as hiding their true identity, ignoring the B in LGBTQIA+.

Kamal told me how he felt this entire story was made 'purely as an excuse for Ryan Murphy to write in a scene where male bisexuality is dunked on by a beloved character (Kurt)'. He told me that this was followed by an interview where Ryan Murphy stresses the importance for gay kids to have Blaine as representation, despite the fact that there was already a gay character.

Why did Ryan Murphy not use this as an opportunity to

make a bisexual male character? Did he not think it was important for *that* demographic to have representation? While this episode was not written by Ryan Murphy himself, did he not oversee it as executive producer on the show? Did he not see the implications of having such a storyline, or did he just not care? Worse, did he agree with Kurt's comments and hold some of those views himself?

The view that m-spec identities are 'just a phase' is a common idea. Often, people will tell m-spec men that they are just gay, but still in the closet. They will say that m-spec identities are just 'a stepping stone' on the way to 'gaytown'. This will even come from people within the LGBTQIA+ community. Some gay men come out as m-spec first, thinking it is easier, and project their experience on others by informing m-spec people that 'they too used to identify as bisexual' or another m-spec identity. This is something we will touch on more throughout the book.

'Anything that moves' trope

Another trope is the 'Anything that moves' trope, which is fairly self-explanatory (TV Tropes, Anything That Moves). This is when a character is open and willing to have sex or be in a relationship with anyone. The character is often lacking in any barriers, or has fewer restrictions than your average person. This trope isn't necessarily restricted to m-spec people; it is possible for characters to have gender as a barrier but still fall into this trope, but is often used for m-spec characters and can reinforce negative stereotypes.

It is very typical for sitcoms to have a male character who is portrayed as a womaniser. One of the biggest examples is Joey

Tribbiani from *Friends*. This is often referred to as 'the Casanova' trope, although many other tropes come into play here. However, the Casanova still has restrictions on who they are attracted to and who they pursue. The 'anything that moves' character goes beyond the Casanova trope, as all or most of these restrictions are removed.

An example of this is Todd from *Scrubs*. Todd isn't just your standard Casanova trope, he shows time and again that he will prey on absolutely anyone. He makes advances and sexual innuendos to everyone and states outright that he 'accepts all applicants'. In season 5, episode 20, 'My Lunch', this was addressed head on.

In this episode, Carla and Elliot suspect that Todd might be gay. He admits he is, only to backtrack on it later, explaining that he uses it to get women. The episode ends with Todd walking down the hallway, hitting on everyone along the way of all ages and genders. When confronted over what he is, he explains that he's 'The Todd'.

He doesn't state his sexuality outright ('ambiguously bi' strikes again) but it can be assumed from the context that he is m-spec. This representation can help reinforce negative stereotypes of m-spec identities. It is common for people to state that m-spec people are sexually promiscuous, and this is supported by the countless representations such as Todd which portray us as nothing more than greedy sex maniacs.

I should state that there is absolutely nothing wrong with being promiscuous; it is important that we remain sex positive and people should feel free to have this sort of sex life if that's what they desire. But it should not be assumed that m-spec people are automatically promiscuous. And the assumptions that follow on from this, such as m-spec people are all cheaters, can prove damaging. I'll be going into this more later in the book.

'Depraved bisexual' trope

A trope that can tie into this is the 'depraved bisexual' trope (TV Tropes, Depraved Bisexual). These are characters that are bisexual or m-spec because, well, why not? They are often cold-blooded, manipulative and murderous and are willing to do anything to achieve their goals, which includes using sex. An example of this is Kathryn from *Cruel Intentions*. Yet again, her identity is ambiguous, she never states that she is m-spec. However, she does make out with Cecile in order to manipulate her.

Another example is Rose from *Get Out*. Again, her identity is ambiguous but she is shown to have been with at least one woman, luring people in so that their family can take over their bodies. This trope paints a negative picture of m-spec people, showing them as people with loose morals, cold and incapable of love.

Impact of negative representation

These tropes bring us back to Shearing's Ramirez Test. Point two on the test asks: 'Is the character's bisexuality presented as a joke or flaw?' (Shearing 2019). When we look at tropes such as the depraved bisexual, it is clear that their m-spec identity is used to portray them as a villainous character while Todd's 'anything that moves' persona is clearly a punchline. These representations fail at the second hurdle of the test.

This leads to a negative image being created around those who are m-spec. Often people will see those who are m-spec as evil or manipulative, as cheaters who will sleep with anyone just for fun. We can be seen as liars, as people who are hiding our true identity or feelings in order to gain something. The negative representation feeds these attitudes and can lead to poor treatment of m-spec people.

What makes representation negative?

I have spent a lot of time here outlining the way in which m-spec people have been represented in media, discussing the tropes and the way in which m-spec identities are discounted and erased or shown in a negative fashion.

But what makes representation negative, exactly? In an episode of the podcast *Two Bi Guys* (2021), Eisner talks about the idea of acceptable representation and how this is often code for respectability. She says the concept of acceptable representation is based around 'the assumption that there is an objective and unified reality to all bi people, that we all share the same characteristics and the same behaviour and that behaviour has to be respectable' (Two Bi Guys 2021).

What this means is that we often demand the representation of bisexual and m-spec people to be 'morally good', that they must act and behave in a way that society deems acceptable. But this is not the reality of m-spec people. M-spec people can be messy, morally bankrupt, amoral or sinful, just like any other human. Eisner says that this demand 'centres non-bi people because it focuses on the question "what will people think about us?" and not "where can we see ourselves?"' (Two Bi Guys 2021).

Eisner says, 'I don't see myself in respectable bi characters' and finds herself more represented by the villains or weirdos (Two Bi Guys 2021). This is incredibly important to discuss. While some may find these tropes damaging or negative, others may see themselves in these characters, more so than the characters who are clean-cut.

I discussed the idea of negative representation with Jacob

Engelberg, a PhD student researching bisexual transgression in film. He told me that when we examine the effect that media has on people, we often make too many assumptions. He asked how we can be sure that people are viewing these images as m-spec or amoral.

I have already previously mentioned how often when m-spec characters have their sexuality go unnamed, they tend to be labelled as either gay or straight by society at large. In a world that deals in the binary, can we really say that these unlabelled characters are seen as m-spec and that this, therefore, informs people of the behaviours of m-spec people?

We also don't know how these characters are being viewed. Can we really say that these characters are seen as 'bad' by the general public? The way in which people perceive certain characters can vary, even when a character is framed as the villain in the story. I've seen numerous conversations around so-called villains in movies or shows where people believe they had a point or side with them.

In Jacob's as yet unpublished thesis, he looks into the case of Basic Instinct, a film from 1992 featuring a murderous lesbian and a murderous m-spec woman. This ignited furore from numerous LGBTQIA+ activists, communities and individuals, who engaged in protests over the film. But while some desired this representation be changed or the film not be shown on the basis that it would fuel anti-LGBTQIA+ sentiment, others embraced this imagery. Some loved how the women in Basic Instinct were strong and empowered and the film showed that LGBTQIA+ people are everywhere and that they will fight back.

Jacob says:

Bisexuality is made meaningful on film when the rules of compulsory monosexuality are transgressed, and these instances often occur through or alongside other social transgressions.

31

I think this connection between bisexuality and transgression helps to explain the amount of 'immoral' depictions of bisexuality we see, but I read those representations as indicating bisexuality's threat to the social order – a threat we should embrace.

When discussing what makes representation good or bad, we must be careful not to fall into the trap of respectability politics, to discount m-spec representation that falls on tropes that are often considered harmful such as the ones I have gone through. For some, m-spec may be a phase, and sexuality isn't something that is always set in stone. M-spec people can be promiscuous, and promiscuity itself shouldn't be seen as a negative trait. M-spec people can be amoral, just as anyone can.

This isn't to say that these images cannot have a negative impact, but it is not so straightforward. The m-spec phobia and erasure that m-spec people receive exist outside these types of representation and while they may inspire this representation (whether consciously or unconsciously) and potentially perpetuate the stereotypes and thereby the discrimination that m-spec people face, there is a level of complexity here that is important to consider.

AIDS and m-spec men

It is not just representation in films and TV that can cause an issue. Representation of m-spec identities is often non-existent in the real world. However, there is a notable example that provided extremely negative forms of representation for m-spec people: the AIDS epidemic.

In 1987, the New York Times published an article on the front page of its newspaper entitled 'AIDS Specter for Women: The Bisexual Man' (Nordheimer 1987). This article outlines the risk bisexual men pose to heterosexual women and how they can pass HIV to the heterosexual community. Even though it is openly admitted early on that the numbers do not show bisexual men as a huge risk, this is brushed aside.

The article dives into the types of bisexual men, portraying them as covert and promiscuous, secretly causing the virus to spread to heterosexual women and even their newborns. This was just one of many articles during the late 1980s that portrayed bisexual men in such a light. This gave rise to what is known as the 'bisexual bridge' theory (Malebranche *et al.* 2010). This is the theory that bisexual and m-spec men are creating a bridge between the gay and straight community, allowing the virus to move between the two.

Articles from *Cosmopolitan* and *Newsweek* were also published in this time period, portraying bisexual men as pariahs and spreaders of the disease (LGBT HealthLink, n.d.). This portrayal was incredibly damaging to the m-spec movement, m-spec men and those who were questioning their sexuality.

This assumption hasn't gone away. Men who have sex with other men are still seen to be at an inherently elevated risk of catching HIV. There are rules and regulations in place, for example, on who can donate blood and they often exclude men who have had sexual intercourse with men in recent history. The US and the UK both have their own restrictions in this regard.

The 'bisexual bridge' theory is still being used today too. The *New York Post* published an article in 2014 headlined 'Women with bisexual partners account for new HIV cases' (Campanile 2014). It states that HIV transmission related to drug use has plunged as a factor, attributing the rise to bisexual men.

As *HIV Plus Mag* states, this 'ignores the reality that HIV transmission can occur between heterosexual men and women' (Brydum 2019). The media tend to ignore this, treating HIV as 'gay cancer', in the words of Todd, a bisexual man I spoke to, said, – a virus that only affects the 'gay community' until they 'inflict it' on heterosexual people.

This demonized male bisexuality, especially among Black men as Black people were also demonized during the AIDS epidemic. In the early 2000s, there were reports on the 'down low' lifestyle, which focused on a 'supposed subculture of African-American men who are secretive about their same-sex encounters' and who then 'bring home' HIV to their female partners (Brydum 2019). Dr Herukhuti, 'a Brooklyn-based cultural studies scholar, sexologist, and educator who identifies as a polysexual black cisgender man', states that this is a 'sexist and racist assumption' that 'disempowers Black women' and 'demonizes Black men', ignoring the systemic issues that are prevalent in our societal structures (Brydum 2019). Medical neglect, access to information and resources, and numerous other structural issues play a huge role in HIV infection. The framing of this 'down low' lifestyle is inherently racist and anti-Black as it ignores these issues, instead treating it as a medical and moral failure of Black people.

Dr Herukhuti also discusses the implications of culture blaming when it comes to new HIV infections, how it leads to both misinformation and stigma, which only worsens the issue. This can be incredibly damaging, especially for already marginalized groups.

Friedman, a researcher who works in this field, agrees, noting that decades of 'unchallenged assumptions' have created a 'complicated, multilayered closet that makes being honest about one's HIV status or sexual orientation difficult' for bisexual people, especially bisexual men of colour (Brydum 2019).

This negative representation creates stereotypes that become ingrained in society and directly cause harm to m-spec people. This was true for Kamal, who was physically attacked by a straight guy when he learned that Kamal was bisexual rather than gay. Kamal told me that this straight guy stated, 'Guys like you are the reason innocent women get AIDS.' He told me that being a Black bisexual man means his body is constantly seen as a risk factor for HIV. He noted that there appears to be a 'specific kind of hostility' from straight men, men who may be quietly homophobic but will be 'openly aggressive towards bisexual men'. He suggested that this may stem from the possibility that women may be happier with bisexual men, thus making the straight man 'less manly' than 'a queer guy', causing their violence to spill over the top. This concept of masculinity is something we will delve into more throughout the book.

This treatment comes as no surprise when you consider the image the media has built over the decades. It is clear that not enough is being done to remove the stigma placed on men who have sex with men, especially Black m-spec men like Kamal. The conversation around the stigma of HIV often doesn't go far enough, staying on a broad level rather than discussing the unique impact on m-spec men and the effect it can have on their coming out. This is a topic we will delve into more later.

Negative education

Negative education plays a role here as well. On the AIDS epidemic, it is not just about portraying m-spec men in a negative light – for many this may have been their first encounter with these identities. The information within these articles misinformed people about these identities, educating them incorrectly, which leads to the harm we saw for Kamal.

According to SIECUS in 2020, nine states explicitly require LGBTQ people to be portrayed negatively (SIECUS 2020). The uneven education in the US means that while students in one part of the country may feel supported and affirmed, students in another may suffer discrimination and shame over their identity.

Religion

Numerous m-spec men that I spoke to noted their religious upbringing and the role it played here. While it did not provide them with any education around m-spec identities, it did inform them on homosexuality, namely that it is a sin. This naturally impacts m-spec men just as it does gay men and other people in the LGBTQIA+ community.

J told me he was taught that 'any attraction towards the same sex is frowned on' and 'would result in eternal damnation'. This has, naturally, impacted him. He told me how he tried to act straight and would fight his attraction to men in an effort to bury his feelings. Quinn had a similar experience growing up in a hyper-religious environment, being told that homosexuality is a sin.

Blizzb3ar also had a similar experience. Blizzb3ar is the son of an elder minister, and religion was a big part of his life. He told me that when he first started dating guys, he kept it a secret. Homophobia was constantly pushed onto Blizzb3ar as he grew up with the idea that you would go to hell if you lay with a man. Numerous people in his school also went to his church, so he didn't want them to know as he didn't want their judgement and to be told that what he was doing was against God. He also told me that this was one reason why he never labelled himself as he didn't want to accept his identity because of his religion. He found himself constantly doubting his identity and existence because of this.

Explicit representation and improvements to education

The issue of representation of and education about m-spec identities may not be perfect, but it has been improving over the years. The GLAAD *Where We Are On TV* report from 2019–2020 found that there were 128 bisexual+ regular and recurring characters on screens. Some of these have been portrayed incredibly well and tick off all points on Shearing's Ramirez Test.

Rosa Diaz from *Brooklyn Nine-Nine* is one such example. She is only seen to date men prior to her character coming out on the show. The show sensitively deals with her storyline where she comes out to her family and then shows her in relationships with women. To make this representation even better, Rosa is played by Stephanie Beatriz, who is bisexual in real life.

Jane The Virgin has not one but two bisexual characters. One is Adam, played by Tyler Posey, a bisexual man who is a love interest for the titular character Jane. They show his coming out to Jane and use it as a teachable moment to explain bisexuality to the audience through Jane asking questions. The other is Petra, played by Yael Grobglas, a bisexual woman and one of the main characters of the show. She has previously been in relationships with men before finding herself attracted to women. Instead of doing a 'straight to gay' storyline, they make her come out as bisexual.

David Rose, played by Daniel Levy, in *Schitt's Creek* doesn't explicitly state his pansexuality, instead opting for a wine analogy where he states he 'likes the wine, not the label'. While this may fall short on the Ramirez Test, they do show David in different relationships with people of different genders to make it even clearer.

Sex Education has provided multiple LGBTQIA+ characters of different genders and races in its three seasons. In season 2, Adam Groff, played by Connor Swindells, comes out as bisexual while Ola Nyman, played by Patricia Allison, comes out as pansexual. The show is still ongoing, so it will be interesting to see where they take these two characters, but having a pansexual woman of colour and a bisexual man is incredibly positive.

Education has been improving as well. In 2019, the UK government announced new regulations for relationship and sex education (Stonewall 2019). This stated that from September 2020, schools in England must deliver LGBTQ+ inclusive education, including different family types at primary school level and different sexual orientations at secondary school level. While this was just for England, Scotland required LGBTQ+ inclusive education from 2021 and Wales from 2022.

In the US, in 2019, Illinois passed a bill that mandated teaching LGBT history from July 2020, making it the fourth state to do so (Schwartz 2019). There is a lot of work to be done in the US though, and since there is no countrywide policy, some states could be moving forwards while others could be going backwards.

Outside traditional education in schools and representation on screens, there are numerous online platforms that m-spec people have flocked to in order to create their own content and help to educate and create positive representation. J.R. Yussuf is a Black bisexual man who created a YouTube channel, *Just J.R.* which focuses on educating people about bisexual and m-spec issues, especially those faced by m-spec men and m-spec people of colour like himself. He has also collated content around bisexual and m-spec men under his hashtag #BisexualMenSpeak.

The AmBIssadors is a YouTube channel I co-founded with Lo Shearing, where we release videos once or twice a month around various bisexual and m-spec issues. We discuss topics like discourse online, the AIDS crisis, bi history and so much more. It has been on a bit of a hiatus as of late (book writing is a lot of work), but there is plenty of content available.

The podcast *Two Bi Guys*, created by two bisexual men, Alex and Rob, discusses lots of issues faced by bisexual and m-spec men. They also interview numerous people from within the community to discuss their work and a topic that they are passionate about.

Vishaal Reddy, a bisexual Indian American man, created a dark comedy series called *Insomnia*. He plays the lead role in this series about a queer Indian American going through an identity crisis. The show touches on topics like mental health, sexuality and racism.

So while mainstream spaces may not be giving us a platform to express ourselves, we are creating content on our own that is inclusive and explicit about our identity as a way to educate, inform and entertain. We are plugging the gaps that institutions and media are creating in order to give m-spec men and people in general visibility that they can relate to.

The impact of poor and sparse representation of and education about m-spec identities has a profound impact on m-spec men. It can prevent m-spec men from coming out, hinder their dating life and negatively impact their mental health. This situation can worsen for m-spec men who hold multiple different marginalized identities, such as being a person of colour. It is so important that m-spec men have a space to build a network, access resources and get support, but is this readily available to them in the same way as other members of the LGBTQIA+ community?

In the coming chapters, I will be addressing these various topics and delving into numerous m-spec men's personal experiences with the problem at hand.

CHAPTER 2

Coming Out

Coming out is no easy task for any member of the LGBTQIA+ community. There is a fear that coming out and expressing your identity opens the door to a world of bigotry. There are a huge number of risks involved when coming out: your family may not accept you and you could become homeless, your school or workplace could become a toxic environment, and treatment from healthcare professionals could change. In the UK, hate crime towards the LGBTQIA+ community has been on the rise (Francis 2020), and similar statistics have been seen in the US (Chibbaro Jr. 2019).

So it comes as no surprise that some people in the LGBTQIA+ community do not come out or are not completely open with those they are close to. Stonewall (2018a) statistics show that 80 per cent of LGB people and 76 per cent of trans people are out to someone in their family, while 46 per cent of LGB people and 47 per cent of trans people are out to everyone in their family. However, these averages disguise the disparities between different groups in the community, and when looking specifically at bisexual people, the statistics change drastically.

For bisexual men, only 14 per cent are out to everyone in their family, while 46 per cent are out to no one. When compared to gay men, where the statistics are 59 per cent and 10 per cent respectively, the issue becomes apparent. These statistics are replicated in the US. According to a report by Pew Research Center (2013) only 28 per cent of bisexual people said all or most of the important people in their life were aware they were LGBT. This figure is way below the average of 54 per cent, and even further below that of gay or lesbian people, where the numbers were 77 per cent and 71 per cent respectively. When looking specifically at bisexual men, the number drops to 12 per cent.

It is clear that m-spec people face increased barriers when coming out. The impact of m-spec phobia and erasure is not to be underestimated here. M-spec people have to tackle both of these on top of homophobia, which is in itself difficult to overcome.

The lack of representation and education, as discussed in the previous chapter, has a real impact here. As we saw, representation of m-spec characters has increased over the years but the historical lack of representation and education held people back from understanding who they were and what it meant to be m-spec. Data from the Pew Research Centre (2013) shows that bisexual people first thought, knew and told someone about their identity at higher ages than gay men (although slightly lower or on par with lesbians).

While representation and education have increased, this hasn't always necessarily been good. Negative representation and education can help reinforce stereotypes around m-spec identities, creating barriers to coming out. According to the *Invisible Majority* report (Movement Advancement Project 2016), 44 per cent of bisexual youth reported online harassment. This is compared to 20 per cent of straight youth and 30 per cent of gay and lesbian youth. According to Stonewall (2018b), 34 per cent of bisexual university students felt excluded by others compared to just 18 per cent of lesbian and gay students. This exclusion and harassment is what stops m-spec people from coming out – it is exactly why they hide their identity.

Unfortunately, the m-spec phobia carries over to LGBTQIA+ spaces. According to Stonewall (2018a), 18 per cent of bisexual men said that they experienced discrimination in their local LGBT community because of their sexual orientation, compared to just 4 per cent of gay men. This is likely why 50 per cent of bisexual men state that they never attend LGBT specific venues and events. Why attend these spaces when you'll just be met with the same confusion, the same questions, the same abuse? How can m-spec people get the help and support they need when the networks and resources made for them also exclude them? Of course, there are likely to be a number of other issues at play which prevent m-spec men from accessing these spaces, but discrimination plays a part here.

In this chapter, we are going to going to delve into the topic of coming out. We are going to look through the lens of people's own experiences with this struggle and work out how to overcome these issues.

Monosexism

As I touched on in the representation and education chapter, sexuality is often defined as a binary concept. This issue is known as monosexism and is best described as the structural privileging of monosexual identities and behaviours (Eisner 2013). It is monosexism that creates this binary concept of sexuality in society, that monosexual identities (that is, gay and straight) are the only real identities.

Monosexism is the reason why education about the spectrum of sexuality and sexual fluidity is so lacking and why representation of these experiences is historically not found. It is responsible for some of the tropes we saw, such as the straight to gay, and why m-spec identities often aren't considered despite the characters' experiences.

Monosexism is the structure that creates the erasure that directly leads to the oppression of m-spec people and the m-spec phobia we experience. It also causes internalized m-spec phobia and erasure. This binary notion of sexuality is so ingrained in our heads that we struggle to understand our own feelings. And due to the lack of, or poor, education on the topic and the non-existent representation, we are unable to deconstruct this notion, forcing us to bottle up part of our attraction by picking a side, straight or gay.

This creates one of the biggest barriers for m-spec men coming out. M-spec men lack the knowledge that these identities even exist. Like myself, most m-spec men I spoke to weren't aware of any m-spec identities when they first started experiencing attraction to multiple genders. Monosexism created a complete lack of representation and education on m-spec identities, which meant there was a gap in my vocabulary. This caused me to struggle with my feelings of attraction. I felt confused, going between straight and gay every time an attraction to different people presented itself. Neither one of these labels made sense in my head, but they're the only ones I knew existed. I found myself coming up with excuses or reasons to ignore or deny part of my attraction, namely my attraction towards men, in order to fit into one of these labels.

James P had a similar experience, holding attraction to people of different genders, but wasn't consciously aware that this attraction was occurring simultaneously. He told me that he assumed it was a 'to-and-fro' while his 'hormones settled down'. Each time he found himself attracted to a woman, or in a relationship with one, he was able to convince himself that he was straight. The denial of his attraction towards men was constantly reinforced. This is a struggle I can relate to, as I often explained my thoughts away as 'puberty' and found reassurance from my attraction to the girls at school.

Living in a monosexist society means that the internalized m-spec erasure can continue even on learning of these identities. As mentioned previously, I first experienced attraction to multiple genders from the age of ten but didn't know any m-spec identities existed until I turned 17 and learned the word bicurious. However, at this point, the binary construct of sexuality was already deeply ingrained in my head, as well as those of my peers.

Hearing people ridicule the identity or dismiss it only caused the doubt over the validity of m-spec identities to increase further in my mind. I couldn't see m-spec identities as real, only straight and gay. Even though I now knew the existence of m-spec identities, it only caused the binary construct of sexuality to be upheld further in my head. I still couldn't make sense of my attraction to multiple genders and as a result I continued to bottle up my attraction to men.

Monosexism creating a binary construct of sexuality often means that m-spec is seen as a combination of parts, a meld of straight and gay, rather than an identity in its own right. People often ask m-spec people questions, such as which gender they are more attracted to (assuming that they have a gender preference), as a way to understand which sexuality they actually are or are more closely aligned to. Some people just assume that m-spec people are actually straight or gay. There are a few concepts that come out from this.

It's all a phase

The first is the idea that m-spec identities are nothing more than a phase. Many believe m-spec people to be confused, undecided, not knowing whether they are actually gay or straight. They believe that m-spec people will eventually figure out their actual sexuality and will make this choice and settle down with someone of the gender they have decided they are actually attracted to.

Essentially, people believe m-spec identities don't hold a state of permanence like monosexual identities do. They believe that once an m-spec person gets into a relationship, they have made that choice and are now gay or straight. This concept quite obviously stems from monosexism – that only gay and straight identities are real.

When m-spec people get into a relationship, their attraction to other genders doesn't disappear. The relationship may not work out and the m-spec person's next relationship could be with someone of a different gender. There is also an assumption of monogamy there. The m-spec person could be polyamorous and engage in more relationships with people of varying genders.

This concept can become internalized within m-spec people and damage their perception of m-spec identities. I spoke to Kamal, a bisexual man, who told me that his understanding of gay and straight 'didn't really correspond to an attraction pattern so much as who you married'. This meant that he didn't affix a state of permanence to bisexuality, believing that he would 'eventually settle down into either fancying men or women'. He thought that everyone had a 'broad range of attractions' and, similar to how The Sims 2 video game operated, eventually you would find that one person and would only be attracted to them.

This is m-spec as a phase at its very core, believing that people eventually settle into one or the other. Of course, sexuality is fluid. People may find themselves identifying as m-spec and, as time goes on and they gain new experiences, may decide to identify as otherwise. But this doesn't mean that m-spec identities in their entirety are just a phase people go through. Plenty stay identifying as m-spec throughout their entire lives.

Straight passing privilege

The second concept to discuss is that of straight passing privilege. This is the idea that someone who identifies as LGBTQIA+ could be perceived as straight by society and therefore move through society without experiencing hardship, meaning they experience discrimination to a lesser degree, if at all, compared to LGBTQIA+ people whose identity is much more visible.

This idea is often attributed generally to all m-spec people. This is due to the aforementioned idea that m-spec people are a combination of gay and straight. People think that we can simply choose to be straight and therefore become safe from the discrimination and violence that LGBTQIA+ people experience.

By 'choosing to be straight', people think that we can just get into a conventional, so-called heterosexual relationship and be happy. So, for m-spec men, we could get into a relationship with a woman whom we experience genuine attraction towards, fall in love, marry them and be happy. This differs from gay men who get into a relationship with a woman only in order to hide their identity and don't experience any attraction to them.

M-spec men getting into a relationship with a woman makes them appear as a straight person and therefore grants them safety. Because of all this, some believe that m-spec people have it easier. In fact, some gay men come out as m-spec first, despite knowing they are gay, as they believe that by still showing attraction towards women, they are relatively safe.

However, this clearly isn't true. We saw from the statistics earlier that m-spec men are less likely to come out as gay men, which is due to the increased barriers that arise from living in a monosexist society. We struggle to understand our identity and experience m-spec phobia and erasure, on top of homophobia, on coming out.

M-spec men in a relationship with a woman may appear straight but they are still m-spec, which comes with unique struggles. These m-spec men may not be out to their partner for fear of experiencing discrimination, which is something mono-sexual people don't consider. They could be closeted, suppressing their identity, which will naturally affect their mental health.

People may wonder why it is even necessary for m-spec men to come out to their partner if their partner is a woman and they are in a monogamous relationship. But their identity is an important part of who they are and there is a fear that they could express something that would reveal their attraction and cause their relationship to fall apart. This is a topic I will be discussing more in the next chapter.

J told me how he sometimes had thoughts about just getting into a relationship with a woman. That way, he wouldn't have to come out and everything would be okay. But he knew that, deep down, he still wouldn't be himself. He would be denying his identity.

Secretly gay

The third concept is the idea that m-spec men are actually gay. This, in some way, directly contradicts the last concept.

As mentioned, people who are m-spec are often seen as either actually straight or actually gay. When it comes to m-spec men, most often we are assumed to be actually gay but in denial, rather than straight. It is the opposite for m-spec women, who are seen as actually straight and only get together with women to gain the attention of men. M-spec non-binary people and people of other genders tend to be erased entirely – in a world that works in binaries, both their gender and their sexuality don't make sense.

The reasoning for this is due to phallocentrism – the idea that the penis is the central element in society. When discussing sexuality, it is the relationship that one has with the penis that determines one's sexuality.

This idea is discussed by Miki R. in *Recognize* (R. 2015) along with how phallocentrism plays a role in bisexual invisibility. In his text, he talks about the erasure of bisexual men and bisexual women as gay and straight respectively, and how our relationship with penises causes this issue.

Miki R. discusses his own experiences with bisexual invisibility and how easy it is to claim a gay identity just by expressing a desire to touch someone else's penis, but impossible to claim a straight identity (even though he has no desire to do so). Bisexuality in men is often not recognized and when it is, it is often seen as 'just another flavor of gay because the defining aspect of us is that we touch dick' (R. 2015, p.171).

A desire for or contact with vaginas doesn't matter or is seen as irrelevant. It does not play a part in determining a person's sexuality. And this is not just on a sexual level, as Miki R. elaborates. This is on an emotional and intellectual level as well. It is the relationship and bond a man has with those who have a penis that determines their sexuality. Having an emotional connection with them makes you gay and a lack of that makes you straight. Vaginas are completely invisible and play no factor in this.

This explains why m-spec women are often seen as straight too, and even why they are seen as playing with women for the attention of men. It is centring the penis in their attraction, in the sexual relations between two women. It is as if sex between two women is not understood as there is a lack of penis involved.

Phallocentrism is very cisnormative, very heteronormative and very binary in notion, which is to be expected in our society, which is all of those things. It is borne out of our patriarchal society that centres cis men above all else. As you can see, phallocentrism is the cause of a lot of the erasure m-spec people receive and why m-spec men are most often seen as gay.

Monosexism and phallocentrism create a denial of multi-gender attraction in men, painting them as closeted gay men who are confused and undecided. The lack of education plays a big role in holding back m-spec men in their journey to self-realization and coming out. Having representation never consider m-spec identities, showing it as a phase or something undefined, only helps to reinforce these ideas in society.

Statistics from Global Dating Insights (White 2016) show that bisexual men realize their identity at a much later age than gay men. The lack of knowledge and awareness of m-spec identities is directly responsible for this difference.

Of course, as mentioned previously, this is only one side of the coin. Negative representation and education is the other. Showing m-spec people as cheaters or as vectors of disease can build a negative image of these identities that mean that even those men who understand their identity as m-spec refuse to come out. They may be scared of how others will see them, the reaction they may get. Or they may be ashamed of their identity and wish themselves to be different, to be straight.

And it is not only the negative portrayal of m-spec identities that impacts us. The negative connotations of homosexuality and being gay also affect us.

Living in a heteronormative society means we learn that being straight is the norm and anything outside this is othered, seen as wrong or bad. These ideas can cause m-spec men to suppress their desires and attraction towards men and stop them from being their full selves.

All of this combined is what causes the poor coming out rates of m-spec men that we touched on at the start of this chapter and the disparities between m-spec men and gay men.

School

As mentioned in the previous chapter, education about LGBTQIA+ identities is not something that has historically been conducted in schools. In the UK, teaching students about LGBTQIA+ identities was outlawed for over a decade, from 1988 to 2003 (2000 in Scotland), due to the fact that it was seen to be promoting homosexuality and indoctrinating vulnerable kids (LGBT History Month, n.d.).

The Local Government Act was not clear as to what exactly constituted a breach, and there was uncertainty around whether schools were included or if it was only applicable to the content produced by local councils. However, the fear of being in breach of Section 28 meant that many erred on the side of caution. This led to LGBTQIA+ student support networks being shut down and confusion about the support teachers could provide to students who were experiencing homophobic bullying.

While Section 28 of the Act was repealed in 2003, the lack of update to the curriculum to positively teach children about

LGBTQIA+ identities meant that the idea that these identities were abnormal or morally wrong persisted in the minds of many.

While the US doesn't appear to have had its own version of Section 28 (a countrywide ban on educational institutions teaching students about LGBTQIA+ identities), the situation can vary state to state. According to SIECUS (2020), nine states still explicitly state that LGBTQ people must be portrayed negatively and only 11 require positive LGBTQ education. This was the situation in 2020. It can be expected that the situation a few decades prior to this may have been a lot worse.

The poor education about LGBTQIA+ identities in schools means that many people grew up with the understanding that these identities are invalid, wrong or abnormal. Not only did this impact the minds of LGBTQIA+ students, causing harm internally, but it directly contributed to the bullying they experienced at school. It also meant that there was a lack of network and support from teachers and the institution itself to ensure the safety of LGBTQIA+ students, and no proper action taken on the perpetrators of such abuse.

According to Stonewall in 2017, 45 per cent of LGBT students said they had been bullied for their identity and 45 per cent of the students who were bullied had never told anyone. Offensive language was commonplace in schools, with 52 per cent stating that they often or frequently heard homophobic language and 36 per cent stating they often or frequently heard biphobic language. The students often felt as if they had nowhere to turn, with 53 per cent saying there wasn't an adult at school they could talk to, and only 29 per cent of those being bullied had teachers intervene.

The situation is similar in the US. Statistics from the Human Rights Campaign show that 29 per cent of bisexual youth were often or frequently verbally harassed, 28 per cent experienced being called slurs frequently and 7 per cent reported being physically assaulted frequently or often at school (Andre *et al.* 2014). It was also seen that m-spec youth were less likely to come out, both to family and friends and in school, whether that be to teachers or classmates. This means that they may not be able to get the support or help they need, should it even exist.

I often experienced people calling me 'batty boy' at school. This is a term that originated in the Caribbean and is often used as an offensive way to refer to homosexual people. I am perceived to be quite feminine and this was the case while I was at school too. This is due to the upholding of traditional gender roles and archaic stereotypes. Because of my supposed lack of masculinity, there was an assumption among those in my school that I was gay and I was ridiculed because of this.

The idea that femininity in men is evidence of their homosexuality has been discussed in numerous places. Kate and Deaux (1987) discuss stereotypes and implicit societal belief in the inversion theory. The inversion theory is that some young people identify so strongly with their parent of a different sex to theirs that they take on their characteristics. This also means that they are sexually attracted to the same sex. So for men, this means displaying feminine characteristics and being homosexual.

While it is said that the 'relationship between masculine and feminine personality traits and sexual orientation is extremely weak' (Kate and Deaux 1987, p.84), there is an implicit belief of this theory in society. That is to say, there is a societal belief that homosexual men display feminine characteristics. There are studies that prove this societal belief, showing that people believe the traits of homosexual men to be more closely aligned to the average woman, and likewise men who display feminine characteristics are perceived to be homosexual.

The concept of masculinity in society is constructed around

white cisallohet able-bodied men and, as a result, men of colour and disabled men are more likely to fall outside this. This can be seen in the way Asian men are so often feminized in society and disabled men are less likely to be able to adhere to the requirements of masculinity, such as being physically strong. The implicit inversion theory within society, therefore, has elements of white supremacy and ableism.

McCreary discuss the idea of the male avoidance of femininity (1994). They talk about how men are viewed negatively and punished harshly for their gender role transgressions. They reason that this could be due to the implicit inversion theory in society. They believe that due to the homophobia that is prevalent in society, men will avoid femininity to avoid being perceived as gay. This can explain why feminine men, such as how I was and am perceived to be, often receive homophobic bullying despite not being out as gay.

This is not an experience I had alone. Polis told me that he was assumed to be gay because he liked Disney and had a friend who was perceived to be feminine. Xy also experienced this: their lack of sporting ability coupled with their interests in music and theatre and mainly hanging out with women meant their masculinity and sexuality were often called into question. Both Xy and Polis stated that they were on the receiving end of homophobic bullying, despite neither of them being out as m-spec or any LGBTQIA+ identity.

I was not out at school, as I did not come out until I was 24. However, I did see homophobia and m-spec phobia at school, and even experienced it myself. Growing up, I heard a lot of people use 'that's so gay' or 'you're so gay'. This was often used as a negative synonym, denoting something as bad or crap. This is still commonplace in schools, with Stonewall showing that 86 per cent of LGBT pupils regularly hear these phrases used at school (2017). The use of these phrases feels like a direct exten-sion of the image that has been created of gay and LGBTQIA+ identities being wrong. Both Polis and Xy, as well as numerous other people I spoke to, heard such phrases and were acutely aware that gay was bad, negative and not something you wanted to be.

The first time I learned about bisexuality was in secondary school (technically sixth form, but I remained at my secondary school for this), where someone had come out as bicurious. They were mocked for this, with everyone stating that they were actually a lesbian and should just admit it. This proved to be a blocker to coming out for numerous people I spoke to. The lack of knowledge, as mentioned earlier in this chapter, meant people weren't aware of any m-spec labels when they first started experiencing these feelings. This caused a great deal of confusion, which unfortunately didn't dissipate on learning of the existence of these terms.

Polis told me how he knew that bisexuality wasn't believed, which prevented him from coming out earlier than he did. He also internalized this issue, that bisexuality and m-spec identities weren't real, meaning he often doubted himself and thought himself deluded about his bisexuality, something I myself experienced and others also expressed.

The anti-gay sentiment within schools also prevented numer-ous people I spoke to from coming out. Ben told me how he thought he would become an even bigger target for bullying and mockery, as LGBTQIA+ identities were often the subject of humour and shame. Xy also expressed this and worried that they would be bullied out of school.

The people I spoke to who did actually come out at school were subject to m-spec erasure, m-spec phobia and homophobia. Cee told me that they initially had a positive reaction from their friend but later received a torrent of abuse from their classmates. Cee was told that bisexual men didn't exist, to stop being greedy and to pick a side. Cee said that they constantly received derogatory and dismissive comments and were made to feel like a freak.

Both Matt and CJ Connor had mixed reactions. While they received some supportive comments, they also received some backlash. Worse, this came from people they considered friends at the time. Matt said that some of his friends started questioning his sexuality, asking why he was claiming to be bisexual when he was actually gay. Meanwhile CJ Connor fell out with some of their more conservative friends.

Xy was outed later at college, where they received more directed public abuse. They were running for student council and found that the posters were defaced, with 'Vote Batty' written under their name.

Everyone I spoke to told me that there was little to no support at school for LGBTQIA+ students. There was very little awareness created around these identities and almost no one came out. For those who did, there were no groups and no support network. Very little, if any, action was taken on the bullying, and a few people I spoke to told me that they didn't see the point in reporting these incidents.

CJ Connor told me that one of the teachers who knew about his identity actually lectured the class for an hour straight about how 'homosexuality would be the downfall of society like it was for the Greeks and Romans', while John found his teachers stopped talking to him and refused to engage or support him. James said that after telling the social, physical and health education (SPHE) teacher about him being trans, he was asked whether that meant he had 'girl bits and boy bits'.

Cee said that Section 28 meant that he was unable to seek the help he needed as teachers weren't able to talk about LGBTQIA+

issues. Xy told me that the anti-gay sentiment in school wasn't just from the students but from the school itself. They went to an all boys' school and it was an unspoken rule that anyone caught in a homosexual (or same-sex) relationship would be expelled and anyone who was openly not straight would be asked to leave 'for the good of the school'.

Mikey told me that he was being bullied at school and that prompted him to speak to the designated support worker at his school about the issues he was facing. Mikey found that faer bisexuality was completely dismissed by the support worker as well as the bullying fae faced from kissing someone of the same sex. The support worker stated that the bullying fae experienced could have happened if Mikey had kissed a dog. The connotation here, likening same-sex attraction to bestiality, is utterly abhorrent.

How can students get the help and support they need when the teachers themselves are ignorant or bigoted, when the rules of the school, or even the law itself, prohibit LGBTQIA+ identities from being spoken about or even existing? It is clear that the education system failed m-spec and LGBTQIA+ students in numerous ways, which had a great impact on their life.

University

The education we receive as we mature plays such a fundamental part in shaping our world view. Educational institutions, such as schools, play such a big role in providing this education. These teachings at the lower levels of schooling greatly influenced these children, causing them to take this understanding of LGBTQIA+ identities into higher education, the workplace and wider society.

The *University Report* from Stonewall (2018b) shows that 33 per cent of LGBT people experienced negative comments from other students and 14 per cent experienced negative comments from a member of staff because of their identity; 34 per cent of bisexual students felt they were excluded by other students compared to just 18 per cent of lesbian and gay people. As a result, 22 per cent of bi students said they weren't open with anyone about their sexuality, compared to 5 per cent of gay and lesbian students.

As mentioned previously, I wasn't out during my time at university. While I saw that some people were accepting of LGBTQIA+ identities, monosexism had caused me to internalize the binary construct and I couldn't accept my identity. I found, as mentioned previously, that people who were accepting of gay people could still be dismissive of m-spec identities. This was the case with my housemate, who dismissed m-spec identities when I brought them up when watching 90210 but was accepting and supportive of our other housemate, who was gay.

R, however, did come out at university and while he initially had a positive experience, this slowly started to turn. R came out to his housemates and they were all supportive at the time, but when he returned from a year abroad he discovered that these housemates were making homophobic and m-spec phobic jokes about him behind his back. R was struggling quite a lot with his mental health at the time and this made the situation a lot worse, especially when he discovered that his housemates were joking about this as well, along with his weight.

R found that his living situation had become an unwelcoming place to be. His housemates would tell R that he was making up his sexuality or just trying to get attention. They would ask probing questions about his sex life or who he fancied, continually putting him on the spot in order to humiliate him.

Fortunately, it appears that the network of support and resources at university is much better than what is available at schools. R was able to get on the wellbeing counsellor service at his university and got a counsellor who was a gay man. The counsellor was able to help R come to terms with what he had been through and provide the support R so desperately needed.

Others I spoke to talked about how university allowed them to meet other LGBTQIA+ people, including m-spec people, make friends, get support and come to terms with their sexuality. Blizzb3ar told me that his university was very queer and it was here that he first discovered bisexuality. He said that he met someone who used that label and, after having a conversation with them, realized that he related to it. After that, Blizzb3ar started using the term and found himself very supported in that. He also found that the wellness centre at university was very supportive of LGBTQIA+ people and had information and resources for LGBTQIA+ people, such as how to practise safe sex.

However, this wasn't the case for everyone. Shae told me that during their time at university, LGBTQIA+ often meant same-sex attracted, and m-spec people were often treated as tourists. He felt as if it would be the same if he reached out to the groups at university. They did attend an event run by the LGBTQIA+ society, but felt uncomfortable in this space, like an outsider. There unfortunately wasn't anything specific for m-spec people and they didn't meet any m-spec people in this space.

So it seems as if the university experience often varies for people depending on where they attend. However, it appears that universities do have a lot in place to help and support LGBTQIA+ students, including m-spec students. From wellbeing services to societies and events, some universities have gone further to help cultivate a space that is safe for m-spec people. More of this is needed, and at an earlier stage than university.

The workplace

Statistics from Stonewall show that 49 per cent of bisexual men aren't out to anyone in the workplace (2018c). This is compared to the 18 per cent average of lesbian, gay and bisexual people. It is clear that the barriers to coming out for m-spec men are at play in the workplace. This is not surprising when you consider the experiences of LGBTQIA+ people in the workplace.

Eighteen per cent of LGBT staff stated that they experienced negative comments from their co-workers; 17 per cent experienced exclusion and 18 per cent experienced discrimination when applying for a job, all because of their sexual orientation (Stonewall 2018c). And this is just the tip of the iceberg. Discrimination when it comes to being promoted, abuse from customers and being told to hide their identity are all commonplace for LGBT people in the workplace.

Statistics in the US paint a similar picture, with 58 per cent of bisexual people reporting being exposed to biphobic jobs at work (Movement Advancement Project 2016). As with the UK, 48.8 per cent of bisexual people say they aren't out to anyone at work (Sears and Mallory 2011). And only 44 per cent of bisexual people feel that their workplace is accepting of their bisexual employees, compared to 60 per cent of gay men (Pew Research Center 2013).

'Researchers from Anglia Ruskin University combed through 24 studies that charted the salaries of people in Europe, North America and Australia between 2012 and 2020' (Milton 2021). They found that bisexual men get paid 10.3 per cent less than their straight counterparts, which was worse than the statistics for lesbian women, bi women and gay men.

While some of the statistics in the UK aren't specific to m-spec people, the data along with that from the US makes it clear that m-spec people experience discrimination in the work-place because of their identity. This creates fear, which prevents them from coming out and being their authentic selves at work.

Xy has both seen and experienced a wide variety of dis-crimination in the workplace. They told me that during their holiday jobs growing up, they heard people use homophobic slurs about people they didn't like and witnessed them mock-ing known LGBTQIA+ celebrities. When they were older and actually out, they were often on the receiving end of m-spec phobia. Xy said that people were often doubtful about their identity because they were in a relationship with a woman and some suspected that they were only claiming to be bisexual for the attention.

Some of the worst abuse Xy faced was, upsettingly, at a popular LGBTQIA+ pub/club. They not only received abuse from their colleagues, who were gay, but the clientele as well, who were mostly LGBTQIA+. Since they were married to a woman, numerous people stated that they were lying to their wife. They were accused of lying to get the job, being a cheater, untrust-worthy and secretly closeted. This primarily came from gay men, but they also had run-ins with lesbians, some of whom stated that m-spec men were actually straight and preyed on trusting women.

Seth had similar experiences to Xy in the workplace. They told me how a co-worker would constantly make jokes about how they were straight. When Seth finally decided to call them out on this, they were completely dismissive saying, 'Yeah, whatever, you made out with some guys at a party.' After Seth disclosed his dating history, the co-worker dropped the topic. This shouldn't have had to occur, we shouldn't have to have to prove our identity to anyone. And not having a history of dating or having sex with people of different genders doesn't erode your m-spec identity. If Seth had only kissed a few guys at some parties, that doesn't erase their identity.

Blizzb3ar used to work for the US government and found that a lot of his co-workers had bigoted views. His boss would often make homophobic comments, especially about LGBTQIA+ public figures, such as music artists, who were proudly and unapologetically themselves. His boss would often express how he wished these people wouldn't 'do that in public'. Blizzb3ar wasn't out while he worked as he didn't feel comfortable enough to be himself. In fact, since his job didn't require him to interact with his colleagues, he often kept to himself as he didn't feel comfortable in this environment. Recently, as a result of the attitudes in his workplace and the impact it was having on him mentally, Blizzb3ar quit this job.

Prior to this job, Blizzb3ar used to work at his college and found this environment much better. His boss was queer, he told me, and was incredibly understanding and supportive of Blizzb3ar and his identity.

Friends and family

Coming out to friends and family can be incredibly difficult. On the one hand, these are people you are close to and would expect to love you for who you are. But on the other, there is a fear that coming out could cause these bonds to become strained and result in you losing the people you love. There is a fear that they may have preconceived notions of m-spec identities and hold bigoted ideas on them or queerness as a whole.

For those who are reliant on their family for shelter and financial support, coming out could result in these ties being severed, making you homeless and unable to fend for yourself.

There are very real risks involved when coming out, which hold true for everyone who is LGBTQIA+, not just m-spec men.

However, it is clear that these issues and fear of bigotry and misunderstanding impact m-spec men more acutely than other demographics in the LGBTQIA+ community. As mentioned previously, Stonewall's statistics (2018a) show that only 14 per cent of m-spec men are out to everyone in their family, while 46 per cent are out to no one. This is replicated in the US, where research shows that only 12 per cent of m-spec men say all or most of the important people in their life are aware of their identity.

For me, coming out was incredibly difficult. I was very aware growing up that my parents did not accept homosexuality or queerness and would not be happy if I or any of my siblings turned out to be LGBTQIA+. In fact, they stated this outright when being presented with queerness, whether that be on TV, in the news or in real life. They would make offensive jokes or would state that it was wrong or unnatural.

I already felt that I couldn't be myself, due to my supposed femininity. I was, and still am, quite an emotional person who liked playing with soft toys, enjoyed Nintendo games and didn't work out or play football. This, in the eyes of my peers and family members, made me unmanly and led to the assumption that I was gay.

There was a fear here that if I were to admit my feelings towards men, that would confirm their assumption and cause the ridicule to intensify. Of course, as mentioned earlier, the other part was that gay didn't fit and being labelled as such would only cause further confusion.

Even after coming to terms with my own identity, I was terrified of opening up to my family lest I be rejected or even ousted from my family home. My dad couldn't even accept my supposed feminine behaviours, telling me to 'stop acting like a girl' throughout my youth and continuing to make homophobic jokes. How could I expect him to accept my bisexuality?

When I did eventually come out to my family, I got a very mixed reaction. My siblings and a few of my cousins on my mum's side of the family were very accepting of me and celebrated my identity. My mum, however, not so much. She was shocked at my announcement and on me asking her if she hated me, she responded that she did not, but she wasn't happy. She asked whether this meant I would start dressing like a girl and implored me to just get with a woman.

Quinn had a very similar experience. Quinn originally came out as homosexual biromantic but tended to use the label gay almost exclusively for a number of reasons (which I will get into later). When Quinn came out as bisexual some family members celebrated this. They saw this as an opportunity for Quinn to now enter a relationship with a woman, a so-called traditional relationship.

This is an issue that many m-spec men have to deal with. Not only do we get told we are simply closeted gay men, but are also often pressured to get into different sex relationships, especially by family members. They think that if we do so, they can forget about our identity as it no longer matters. This is simply another form of erasure – our identity doesn't disappear when we enter a relationship.

Todd is a bisexual man who grew up during the AIDS epidemic in the 1980s. He told me that the AIDS epidemic affected his decision to remain closeted during this time. He said that 'as straight women started to be infected with AIDS', there was an assumption 'that secretly bisexual men were cheating on their wives at bathhouses'. This image is what led to bisexual people being portrayed in media as 'devious, dishonest, and recklessly promiscuous'.

While I can't say for certain where these tropes around m-spec characters originated from, you can see the parallels between the portrayal in fictional media and the image that society has created around m-spec people. This can form a vicious cycle that reduces m-spec men to a negative stereotype, prevents people from coming out and decreases the visibility of m-spec men.

Todd told me that in the 1980s, AIDS was 'gay cancer' and there was an assumption that men who have sex with men 'would eventually develop AIDS'. He recalls a moment in the last five years where a family member asked him, privately, if he was still well. From the context, it was clear they were referring to HIV/AIDS. He felt that 'coming out as attracted to other men' at the height of the AIDS epidemic seemed 'unwise' and would have marked him as a 'pariah'.

I never got the opportunity to come out to my dad. I found out not long after coming out to my mum that my dad already knew, having discovered my identity from my social media (despite him not having any social media accounts). A few months later, I discovered that his family, my cousins, had been stalking my social media and outed me to him.

My cousins, my mum's family, who were initially accepting of my identity later revealed themselves to hold some questionable views. One cousin called me gay and, when I corrected them, told me that I was more aligned that way anyway. When I was telling them my mum's reaction, they told me that I had to understand that no one wants their child to be gay and they themselves didn't want their son to be gay.

Kamal told me that just after his 18th birthday, his dad threatened to kill him. This led to Kamal leaving home and being homeless for a few months. Kamal said that he could not be certain that his dad's behaviour was because of his sexuality, as his relationship with him had been bad for a long time and he was unsure if his dad even knew of his sexuality, although he suspects that it was a factor.

Faith

Faith can be an incredibly important aspect for many people. Some may grow up in a deeply religious environment, while others may find spirituality as a way to connect with something greater than themselves. Practising a religion for many involves frequenting a place of worship, where you often interact with a community and may find friendship, form bonds and more.

To find out that you're LGBTQIA+, as a religious person, can be incredibly difficult. Many religions preach that homosexuality and queer acts are sinful and that can create quite a toxic and damaging environment for LGBTQIA+ people.

While this may impact all LGBTQIA+ people, it is again clear that this issue is felt more acutely by m-spec men than other demographics in the LGBTQIA+ community. According to Stonewall (2018a), 64 per cent of bisexual men aren't out to anyone in their faith community, compared to just 26 per cent of gay men.

While society itself is very heteronormative and teaches much the same principles – that is, that same-sex attraction is wrong – this can be intensified for religious people. The negative ideas can become more deeply ingrained and the denial of your attraction even stronger if you are being made to believe that your very soul will suffer the consequences of your sinful behaviour.

This was true for J, a bisexual man I spoke to. He told me that he didn't come out to his family due to religious reasons. He quotes the words his mum told him: 'You can be gay and I'll still love you but I will be very disappointed.' This had a profound impact on him.

J told me how he spent a lot of time and effort trying to fight his feelings for men or bury them somehow, but it proved unsuccessful. To this day, J still feels the need to police himself on his reactions to LGBTQIA+ matters when around family members in case he gives his identity away.

While many talk about how men identify as m-spec before identifying as gay, the reverse is rarely talked about. Because of the lack of knowledge, and negative connotations, of m-spec identities, some m-spec people may come out as gay first. Others could be hiding their sexuality, as mentioned earlier, but not by identifying as straight but gay instead.

As mentioned earlier, Quinn, originally came out as homosexual biromantic but tended to use the label gay almost exclusively, partly due to growing up in a Christian household. While they were taught that homosexuality was a sin, they also grew up in a world of 'heightened purity' where it was constantly drilled into them to not perceive women sexually or romantically. They were told not to kiss or even hold hands until marriage. This actually made it easier for them to embrace their same-sex feelings over their different sex feelings. Another reason they used the gay label was the perceived notion that bisexual was the 'socially acceptable' gay, that it was easier. They felt that gay was more revolutionary in that regard and if they were to tell their family that they were bisexual, the family would pressure them to marry a woman. So it became easier for Quinn to disregard their feelings for women so they didn't have to deal with this.

What we can change

So, what changes do people want to see? When it comes to schools, almost everyone I talked to mentioned that inclusive education is key. This has only recently started changing in the UK, and other countries, such as the US, still have a long way to go on this front. It is also important to ensure that this education focuses on every part of the LGBTQIA+ spectrum, teaching the ins and outs of the different parts of our community. Dedicating time to discuss the different labels in the m-spec community, what they stand for and breaking the well-known stereotypes can go a long way to reduce the stigma.

The other important part here is ensuring that teachers are clued up on LGBTQIA+ identities, issues and the community so they can provide adequate support. Having teachers project ignorance, such as that which James experienced, is just not good enough. Students should be made to feel safe, secure and able to ask teachers questions and find somewhere to get the help and resources they need. Teachers also need to do better than just a general 'don't bully people for being LGBTQIA+', ensuring that they create a safe environment at school and deal properly with those who express bigotry and hatred.

At university level, people mentioned wanting events or groups specifically catering for m-spec people. While this may be available at some universities, it is unlikely to be a universal experience. Ensuring that there is a space for people to be able to express themselves and meet like-minded people without fear of discrimination is so important.

Workplaces should also enact some form of policy, with inclusive language to ensure that m-spec people are included and protected. Making work a place where people can bring their whole selves is so important, so diversity and inclusivity should be a core value of every workplace, and businesses should make sure that these values are understood by every person they hire. Providing onboard training in the importance of LGBTQIA+ identities and issues can help ensure the safety of their employees.

Advice

With all of these difficulties for m-spec men coming out, how can we make it easier for those questioning their sexuality? How can we help those trying to come out? I have spoken to numerous m-spec men to ask for their thoughts and feelings around what they recommend.

Nearly every person I spoke to said that they wished they had come out earlier than they did. But, as James P noted, it's important not to look back on the what-ifs, it isn't useful. It's important to remember you are where you are now and think about what you can do going forward. Today is the day to make that change, so don't put it off.

As a few people suggested, try to enjoy the questioning. Kamal said that there shouldn't be a rush to affix a label to yourself. Exploring is an important part of the journey to help you figure out who you are and what you want. Osh echoed this, urging people to enjoy the journey, and said that there 'is no fixed timing to know' what your sexuality is, 'no matter what anyone tells you'.

Todd felt that experimenting when and where you can is always fun and he talked about how it helped him. It is important here to remember that there is another person involved when experimenting, so communication is key. Make sure that boundaries are set and everyone is on the same page regarding the experience. For example, if it is just a one-time event, make sure that this is clear. It is also important to remember to be safe. Your safety during sex is your responsibility, no one else's. So, ensure that you take the precautions you need to keep yourself safe and get tested.

Experimenting can grant you the space to figure out what works for you, but it isn't for everyone. And you don't necessarily need to have a wealth of experience with people of different genders to validate your identity. As John B said, you can be a virgin or only have had sex with someone of a different gender and still be bisexual. Osh echoed this, stating that 'the attraction is defined by what you feel not what other people tell you'.

It can help secure the feelings you're having internally, but even if you don't enjoy the experience, this doesn't necessarily mean you can't still be m-spec. Quinn told me that it's important to 'give yourself permission to use the label that makes the most sense for you'. There isn't a test you need to pass to prove your sexuality to anyone, and others' views don't matter.

So, where can people go to help understand their sexuality more? There are a lot of recommendations. Online is always a great resource, but can come with issues. Ant said that social media can be harmful 'as it's one person's opinion'. He recommended that people 'reach out to community support and sexual health centres'. There are a lot of organizations that people recommended: Bi.Org, Bisexual Index, Bisexual Resource Center and Stonewall were some of the ones that came up.

As you can see, there are a lot of organizations that cater specifically for m-spec people and provide swathes of content, articles, stories and more that can be good to digest and help you on your coming out journey. They also link to other organizations too, which have even more content.

There are in-person events and community focused groups too; Bi Pride UK and BiCon are two huge events in the UK. There are local community groups too; Bi Community News is a good place to find your local one in the UK. For others, having a quick search online or on websites like Meetup may bring something up. If not, reaching out to one community or organization can normally help you find others.

But some of these places have their own issues. There are several organizations that have fallen into disrepute, including some m-spec organizations. BiNet USA tried to copyright the bi flag and numerous leaders stepped away. Bi.Org has proven to not support pansexual people, erasing pop culture figures and doubling down when called out on social media. BiCon has been called out on their racism and classism, prompting them to make a statement about it but, as yet, very little action has been taken to rectify this.

While it has issues, social media can also be incredibly helpful. Quinn talked positively about Bi Twitter, how incredibly welcoming they were and the positive impact this had on their journey of self-acceptance. I concur with this, as I threw myself into Twitter when I was coming out and it helped me immensely in connecting with the community. But this space can be a minefield, so it is important to navigate it safely.

Try to seek out large m-spec organizations online and see the organizations and people they recommend, the people they follow and the stuff they share. Use that to build a network of your own and slowly connect with the community. You may encounter some people who will invalidate you, but for each one you will find many others granting acceptance. Try not to put too much stock in one person's opinion, or the opinions of bigots. Talk to numerous people and you'll be sure to find those like you.

The same can be said of other social sites, such as Reddit and Tumblr, both mentioned in people's responses. There are good and bad areas to every site, useful content alongside harmful stuff. Bear this in mind when navigating such websites for information and knowledge; not all of it is good. But for those who want to connect with individual people and find others like them, they can be a useful tool.

In a similar vein, YouTube has a ton of content but caution must be taken as there is plenty of negative content there. It's the same with podcasts. *Two Bi Guys* have regular podcasts and the hosts are both bisexual men, which can help m-spec men coming to terms with their sexuality. I also help run *The AmBIssadors*, a YouTube channel focusing on m-spec people and issues. The community online can help guide you to other useful channels and podcasts. Films can also be great, even if they don't necessarily have an m-spec character. J recommended *Moonlight* and *Love, Simon* as two films that helped him come to terms with his feelings

James P noted how useful other people's stories can be too – to hear from real people and understand the experiences they went through. Of course, due to the rates of coming out, there aren't a lot of these and they won't always be positive either. This can add fear, but there are some wonderful positive stories out there. Online blogs and YouTube can again be useful here but there are also a few bisexual anthologies out there too. *The Bi-ble* volumes 1 and 2, published by Monstrous Regiment, are two such books (Desmond and Nickodemus 2017, 2019). There is also *Recognize*, an anthology of works created by bisexual and m-spec men (Ochs and Sharif Williams 2015).

So, once people have the knowledge and understand their sexuality, how do they come out? J recommended to start small, something that many others mentioned too. He said that if you have friends from the LGBTQIA+ community, start with them as they will likely be more understanding and supportive, especially if they are m-spec themselves.

Coming out to family can be tricky. On the one hand, you want them to know the true you. On the other hand, it can lead to troubling consequences, such as being kicked out of home. It's important to have a support system, or a safety net. One person mentions that it may even be worth waiting until you are less dependent on them, as that way you can still support yourself should anything happen.

Everyone agrees that coming out is difficult and the most important thing is to take it at your own pace. There should never be any pressure to come out and if you don't feel safe telling certain people, then don't. That's entirely okay. Ant said that you can still be your genuine self without telling absolutely everyone and it isn't worth the harm, regardless of the idea that 'it gets better'. As Todd says, there is no shame in postponing coming out or just never telling certain people in your life.

Once you are out, own it! John B said to be proud of your identity and embrace your true self. He said that those who truly love you will accept you and always love you for who you are. Being out, loud and proud can also be incredibly powerful. As Alan said, each person who comes out makes it easier for the next person. You can increase visibility, make others feel comfortable and even encourage others to come out too.

All in all, coming out is an incredibly difficult undertaking. If you don't feel comfortable or safe, don't do it. Being able to come out is a privilege that not everyone is afforded. But if you can, do. Take your time, tell people one by one. It will be hard. For some, it is the best thing they have ever done but it doesn't always go well for everyone. There is a community out there but, as alluded to, it has its issues and isn't accessible for everyone, especially those with other marginalized identities. I wish you the best of luck on your journey, whatever you decide to do.

CHAPTER 3

Dating and Relationships

Many monosexual people believe that m-spec people have it easier when it comes to dating and relationships. Our ability to be attracted to more than one gender, all genders or to people regardless of gender would seemingly open the door to more people, more options, when it comes to picking out potential partners. And on the face of it, this would indeed be true.

However, this isn't necessarily the case. M-spec people often have to deal with what is called double discrimination. This is discrimination from 'both sides', from cisallo straight people as well as from the LGBTQIA+ community. This can, in fact, make dating harder for m-spec people. M-spec men are often erased and invalidated from both sides, labelled as 'closeted gay'.

According to Zava (n.d.), 81 per cent of women said that they would not date a bisexual man. I have seen somewhat similar results on social media, such as a poll on Twitter asking women if they would date a bisexual man. This poll got 3429 votes and 42 per cent said no while only 27 per cent said yes. The remaining

31 per cent were simply wanting to see the results, meaning over 60 per cent of the approximately 2300 who actually voted said no.

Straight people refuse to date us as they assume we are gay, while those in the LGBTQIA+ community assume we are 'down low' and closeted. We're told that we are liars and cheaters, indecisive or promiscuous. We're told that we can't be satisfied with just one person, that we will surely stray, are polyamorous or will want to be in an open relationship.

Not all of these assumptions are negative. Plenty of people are in open relationships or are polyamorous, and people should be allowed to sleep around or date or have relationships in whatever way they want. But many see these as negative, they have rigid, traditional western ideals and don't accept those who stray from the norm. The assumption that m-spec people are, by nature, polyamorous also shows a fundamental lack of understanding of what it means to be m-spec and in a relationship.

Others are, quite obviously, negative. And all of these, and more, are used as reasons to not date m-spec men. To avoid us. Those outside our relationships will often erase us as well. Once we are in a relationship, we are seen to have chosen our identity, to have picked our side.

Those who don't know our identity are often shocked to find out and it can lead to m-spec phobia and erasure. People may tell us we're going to hurt our partner or ruin their lives. They may start to probe or ask personal questions about the inner workings of our relationships. We may be said to be a different identity, based on the gender of our partner. It can also mean re-coming out, to people who already knew our sexuality, when the gender of our partner changes. This can be incredibly exhausting.

So, how do you navigate this? How do you date as an m-spec man? When, and how, do you tell the person you are dating about your identity? And how do you deal with the questions, the backlash and negativity? When, and how, do you come out to someone you're in a relationship with and how do you respond if they don't understand? And lastly, how do you cope with outsiders injecting their unwarranted views and opinions on this topic?

In this section, we are going to highlight the struggles m-spec men have to deal with when it comes to dating and relationships, and we will hear some personal stories. We will discuss different types of relationships and comments from those outside the relationship. This will end on some positivity, along with some advice from others on this topic.

Dating women

In the Zava poll (n.d.), it is seen that 81 per cent of women said that they would not date a bisexual man. While it does not provide any explanation for the response these women gave, we can deduce the reasoning behind this result.

M-spec erasure plays a big part here. As discussed in Hertlein, Hartwell and Munns (2016), 'people's discomfort with bisexuality – and the negativity and biphobia that stem from it – are a result of society's conceptualization of sexual orientation as an either/or proposition' (p.4). Society creates a false dichotomy that sexuality is either straight or gay, removing the idea of attraction as a spectrum that can present itself in ways outside this.

So m-spec men could be seen as either straight or gay, but this often isn't the case. As mentioned previously, m-spec men are often seen as closeted gay men rather than straight. Why is this? How does this formulate?

This likely all stems from a combination of monosexism,

phallocentrism and the implicit inversion theory, all concepts I discussed in the coming out chapter. Monosexism is the structural privileging of gay and straight, placing sexuality as a binary construct and systemically erasing m-spec identities as real. Phallocentrism is the concept that people are altered by their attraction or relation to the penis. And implicit inversion theory is the idea that homosexual men are feminine.

What this amounts to is the concept that m-spec men are actually gay. Since m-spec men are attracted to and have sex with men, and since only gay and straight are real identities, they must be gay. If their attraction to women is acknowledged, then the fact that they are also attracted to men will mean they are viewed as feminine or less masculine than a heterosexual man may be viewed. And, as a result, they are seen as less desirable, at least by some women.

This makes a clear link between masculinity and heterosexuality. This is discussed by Hertlein et al. (2016), who say that 'negative attitude toward male same-sex attraction and behavior is a result of the Western notion that masculinity is tied to heterosexuality, and that attraction to other males is antithetical to a masculine identity' (p.5).

This concept is heavily rooted in both heteronormativity and misogyny. The world view is that men are masculine and attracted to women, and women are feminine and attracted to men. For a man to be attracted to another man is to make him more woman-like and thereby feminine. He is seen as lesser as a result because women themselves are seen as lesser.

M-spec men are therefore rejected by women on the grounds that they are actually gay or that they are not a 'real man' as they are also attracted to men.

Blizzb3ar told me that cisallohet women often expect him to be their gay best friend, which highlights how m-spec men are often erased and seen as gay by women. This also shows how 'gay men' are seen as nothing more than accessories to some cisallohet women, rather than actual people. Alex recounted how he was rejected by a woman on disclosing his bisexuality, where she told him that she wanted a real masculine man. This highlights how male attraction to other men is seen as unmasculine.

Zachary recalled a woman he once dated, the friend of a friend who he had been on a couple of dates with. He said that they had really hit it off but after the third date, she ghosted him. He got in touch with the mutual friend to ask what happened, wondering if he had somehow misread the situation. As it turned out, Zachary had opened up to this woman about his bisexuality on their last date and that had freaked her out. His friend told him that the woman felt guilty about telling him that his bisexuality freaked her out, hence the ghosting.

Terrence told me that he had several straight women turn him down for a second date after disclosing his sexuality to them.

What is interesting is that the m-spec phobia and discrimination don't always come from cisallohet women. In Alex's case, the woman was pansexual. Similarly, Blizzb3ar told me how he went on a date with a bisexual woman, only for her to say that she didn't trust m-spec men, that she didn't believe that they existed and the fact that they 'take it up the ass' made them gay.

This shows how the idea of phallocentrism translates directly into the thoughts and opinions that people hold. The fact that this woman believed that a man being penetrated made them gay is phallocentrist ideology. M-spec women also having these thoughts shows how m-spec phobia can be internalized.

The fact that these women believed that m-spec identities could not exist within men and yet found no conflict in identifying as m-spec women reflects the societal image of m-spec identities. M-spec women are not as readily erased as m-spec men in society; however, this isn't due to acceptance. In fact, this is often because m-spec identities in women are more often fetishized, which is arguably worse. M-spec women are seen as palatable because female sexuality is seen to be more passive and existing to serve the desires of men. The male gaze therefore hypersexualizes and objectifies m-spec women's desires (e.g. threesomes with 'unicorns') in ways that leave m-spec women particularly vulnerable to sexual violence.

It is likely that this idea that is pervasive in our society has been ingrained into these m-spec women and internalized. This causes them to project these m-spec phobic narratives onto m-spec men, thereby erasing them and upholding the mono-sexist, phallocentric and misogynistic world view.

Another issue at play here could be race. Alex said that the expectation of masculinity in Black/African American men within their race is greater than their white/Caucasian coun-terparts. Since both he and the woman he had been dating are Black/African American, the expectation for him to be hypermasculine is one factor at play here. Alex informed me that, one year later, this woman started dating a bisexual Asian American man, which is quite interesting and highlights the racial element at play here.

Joseph told me that he has seen, on several occasions, women who see m-spec men as a last resort, their last chance for love. He said that these women act as if they are hopeless if they 'can't even get an m-spec man to date them'. This highlights how m-spec men are often seen by women – they clearly are not interested in dating m-spec men unless they can't find anyone else. The narrative that m-spec people will get with anyone clearly plays a part here and when these m-spec men don't show any interest, these women think of themselves as unloveable.

Another element at play is the fact that m-spec men are seen as undesirable, and therefore should feel lucky to receive attention from women of a higher social status than them.

Dating within the LGBTQIA+ community

LGBTQIA+ people use the same idea – that m-spec men are secretly gay – as a reason to avoid dating m-spec men. They will often be dismissive of m-spec identities, stating that they aren't real and don't exist and all m-spec men eventually come out as gay. This is especially true of gay men.

Numerous gay men have used an m-spec identity on their coming out journey as a stepping stone, to test the waters and gauge the reaction from people close to them. They know their identity as gay, but erroneously believe that being m-spec is easier. They feel that if they receive hardship on coming out, it will be easier to backtrack into the closet and label it as a phase.

Thus, many gay men project this experience onto m-spec men. They believe these m-spec men to be on that stepping stone they were once on and, eventually, they will reach the other side.

Zachary experienced this when he first came out and entered LGBTQIA+ spaces. He told me that he often encountered gay men who were condescending about his identity. He was told by gay men that his identity didn't exist, that he would 'get there', referring to the fact that he would eventually come out as gay, and that they 'were bi too once'.

Because of this idea that we are still closeted and have yet to come out, gay men tend to avoid dating us. They view m-spec identities, and people who identify as such, as confused and believe that m-spec people are still figuring out their identity.

Again, Zachary experienced this, telling me how gay men

wouldn't want to date him as they 'didn't want to date someone who hadn't yet figured themselves out'. He said that it was clear that they 'didn't view his identity as stable' and thought of him as 'confused' and 'closeted'.

M-spec men often have to deal with this erasure from people, even within the LGBTQIA+ community. This makes LGBTQIA+ places feel unwelcoming and unsafe for many m-spec people, a topic we will explore later.

Fetishization

Rejection due to their identity is only one side of the coin for m-spec men. On the other side is fetishization. J.R. Yussuf, in an article for Wear Your Voice (2021), discusses the commentary that 'bisexual men are the best in bed', which he has observed gaining steam recently, and the fetishistic nature of it.

He states that this comment is mistakenly seen as a positive affirmation but is instead centring these men's sexuality as the entirety of their being, in the same way the rejection m-spec men face does. Bisexual and m-spec men are individuals. Whether someone is good or bad at sex is an individual trait and is also entirely subjective. Stating that m-spec men, for the very fact that they are m-spec, are better at sex than straight men is fetishizing and objectifying. This can be incredibly harmful and damaging and could be a contributing factor in the sexual violence m-spec men face – something I will be discussing shortly.

Yussuf, in his article, also discusses some of the other 'supposedly affirming talking points' about m-spec men, including the idea that they are less misogynistic. I believe that this may help explain the fetishization (from this angle at least). While some women may reject m-spec men, believing they are too feminine, others may want m-spec men for this very reason.

In an article from *Cosmopolitan* (2019), there are mentions of how bisexual men are more compassionate or how it's easier to talk to these men about feminism. There are also mentions of how bi men are more open-minded, less squeamish and communicate better. The article does acknowledge that not all bi men are going to be amazing at sex, and some of the women state that they don't necessarily seek out bi men while others are bi themselves and so prefer bi men for that reason. However, this only makes the article stranger. If you can acknowledge that the act of being bisexual or m-spec doesn't necessarily make these men better lovers, what then was the message this article was trying to convey?

While the experiences that these women have are obviously personal to them, reporting on this in such a manner can lend credence to the idea that m-spec men are better at sex. We can see the same assumptions being played with, just spun in a positive light. As Yussuf states, while many m-spec men may have done the work to unlearn misogyny and so on, we are not a monolith. Moving from denying our existence to wanting us for it, solely due to the promise of 'the best sex', is not in fact deconstructing m-spec phobia.

The fetishization that m-spec men face from within the LGBTQIA+ community is somewhat different and presents an interesting new element. In a panel I hosted for Bi Pride UK discussing bi, pan and m-spec men's experiences, Ife stated that the way cis gay men interact with m-spec men can be fetishizing and comes with certain expectations. They went on to say 'cis gay men often expect bi people to be more dominant, to be more aggressive' (Bi Pride UK 2021).

Previously, I have spoken about the idea of phallocentrism and how m-spec men's attraction and interaction with penises results in being viewed as gay – and how this, coupled with the implicit inversion theory, means that m-spec men are viewed as inherently more feminine, often by women. When discussing this, we mentioned how m-spec men's attraction, desire or experiences with vaginas becomes entirely irrelevant. This, however, may not be strictly true.

It seems as if m-spec men's attraction to women and interaction with vaginas can create the assumption, particularly among gay men, that m-spec men are more masculine. Rob told me that he'd had a few guys on apps tell him that they loved the fact that he is bi. Most of the time they couldn't identify why they loved bi and m-spec guys but when they could, it was due to the fact that they thought m-spec men were all masculine and straight acting.

Thom said that they have seen loads of bios on Grindr, a hook-up app for LGBTQIA+ people, saying 'into straight/bi guys', which shows how bi and m-spec identities are often seen as 'straight-lite'. Thom said that they have had a number of fetishizing interactions after stating their identity, from someone responding 'kinky' to receiving creepy grins. Rob had also seen guys on apps think that m-spec men were married, and getting off on that. It is the idea that they are 'turning a straight guy gay' that draws them to m-spec men.

Again, this shows the same assumptions about m-spec men cropping up, but instead of being used as a cause to reject us, it is used to objectify us. Our supposed alignment to straightness gives some people the idea that we are more masculine than gay men and this is seen as an attractive quality. We fulfil a kink, a fantasy, for these gay men to 'turn' us, to steal us from our wives.

I believe that while fetishization is clearly an experience that m-spec men face, it is not as common an experience as rejection. As mentioned previously, due to a combination of structures that exist in our society, m-spec men tend to be seen as gay and closeted and/or unmasculine and therefore undesirable. M-spec women aren't as readily erased but tend to experience fetishization to a greater degree than m-spec men. And due to the binary structure that our society upholds, m-spec people of other genders (such as m-spec non-binary people) are doubly erased.

Sexual violence

According to statistics from Stonewall (2020), 13 per cent of bi people reported experiencing unwanted sexual violence. This is compared to 7 per cent of gay/lesbian people. It was also reported that 12 per cent of bi men experienced intimate partner abuse (Stonewall 2020). Statistics from the Centers for Disease Control and Prevention (CDC) in the US (2010) show that 47 per cent of bisexual men experienced sexual violence, compared to 40 per cent of gay men and 21 per cent of straight men. Thirty-seven per cent of bisexual men reported an instance of intimate partner violence compared to 29 per cent of straight men and 26 per cent of gay men (CDC 2010). In the report from Stonewall (2020), '42% bi respondents felt their sexual orientation might have been a motivating factor in experiencing sexual violence' (p.12).

Sexual violence is a clear issue among m-spec men, and while they are not alone in their experiences, the disparities here show that the problem is more acute among this group. We can see that their sexuality plays a part in this issue. Their perceived lack of instability and indecision around their 'real identity' places m-spec men at risk of sexual violence.

Kamal told me that after he was kicked out of his house, and thereby made homeless, he was sexually assaulted three times. And each time, his sexuality was a factor at play. He was sexually assaulted by a white gay man on two separate occasions, with both men viewing his bisexuality as a challenge as well as racially fetishizing him. Kamal was also sexually assaulted by his white girlfriend, who wanted him to 'prove' he was attracted to her, shortly after the two previously mentioned incidents.

This highlights how structural monosexism and the erasure of m-spec identities puts m-spec people's safety at risk. The issues m-spec men face in regard to dating and relationships don't stop at being rejected or fetishized for their identity – their identity can become the motivating factor in the sexual abuse m-spec men face.

A recent study from Galop (2022) showed that '23.5% of 935 LGBT+ respondents told us that they had experienced sexual violence which they believed was intended to convert or punish their LGBT+ identity' (p.3). For polysexual people, including bisexual and pansexual people, 20.5 per cent said they had such an experience, which was on par with lesbian and gay people (20.4%).

The desire to put m-spec men into a binary category and the disbelief and distrust of their attraction can become the justification for sexually assaulting m-spec men. It can lead to corrective rape or assault as they try to 'convert' or 'fix' these m-spec men, as we saw with Kamal. This is clearly not an isolated incident, but a much wider issue.

Assumptions at play

This constant erasure of m-spec men as closeted gay men makes dating and relationships difficult. They are met with this assumption not only from those they are trying to date or are dating, but from people outside the relationship too. M-spec men are constantly judged by others and are often subjected to uninvited views, thoughts and opinions from people that are rooted in m-spec phobia or m-spec erasure. These can be acquaintances, supposed friends or those close to their partner.

This can occur for m-spec men when they start dating someone of a different gender to their previous partner, or different from those they tend to date. Since the assumption is that m-spec men are secretly gay, they often experience bigotry when dating someone who is a woman or female-presenting. However, m-spec men are also seen to be 'down low' and may experience bigotry from the idea that they will eventually end up with a woman.

This assumption that m-spec men are closeted gay men is not the only issue that makes dating harder for m-spec men. Another factor that comes into play is the perceived promiscuity of m-spec men, and in fact m-spec people in general. Due to the fact that m-spec people are attracted to multiple genders, we are seen as unable to be satisfied by just one person. The assumption is that m-spec people are therefore unable to commit to a relationship and are likely to cheat. We are labelled as duplicitous, untrustworthy and sex-crazed.

People also often assume that m-spec people will want to be in an open relationship or are polyamorous. In our heteronormative society, monogamy is promoted as the only valid way to have a relationship. This paints a negative picture of other ways to be in a relationship, and for m-spec people these negative ideas are mixed in with m-spec phobia.

Monogamous relationships

M-spec people who are monogamous often deal with m-spec erasure. As mentioned earlier, society perceives sexuality as a straight/gay dichotomy. As a result, 'sexual orientation is typically determined by the relation of one's own gender to that of one's partner' (Hertlein *et al.* 2016, p.4). M-spec identities are often seen as a phase, and once we get into a relationship we are seen to have picked our side, gay or straight.

But of course, not all relationships last forever. Which begs the question, what happens to an m-spec person's sexuality when they break up with their partner? If an m-spec man getting into a relationship with another man makes him gay, is he still gay after he's broken up with said man? Has he now picked his side and has to stick with it? Or does he go back to being m-spec?

Monosexual people seem to fail to understand that a person's sexual orientation is retained regardless of their current partner. So an m-spec man in a relationship with another man is still m-spec. He may break up with this man and go on to have a relationship with a woman or a non-binary person.

This lack of understanding on the part of monosexual people often leads to m-spec people having to deal with questioning and confusion that is rooted in m-spec erasure. It can mean re-coming out to people and reminding them of your sexuality and what exactly it means.

This is an experience that Terrence has had to deal with. Terrence has had more sexual and relationship experiences with men than he has with women, which leads his friends to forget that he is actually bisexual and not gay. He told me how when he did mention a woman he found attractive or would like to date, his gay friends could be quite dismissive of that, rolling their eyes at his comments. He believed that this was either because they didn't get it or they didn't believe him.

When Terrence was in a relationship with a man, he often found his identity erased. His friends told him he'd gone 'full gay' and believed he was in a gay relationship, not a bisexual man in a same-sex relationship.

This shows how people believe m-spec identities to be some sort of midway point, a stepping stone, between gay and straight. It shows how people believe that bisexual and other m-spec identities are a combination of gay and straight, rather than their own identity. It is clear that Terrence's friends saw him as 'part gay' and him getting in a relationship with another man then made him 'full gay'.

Of course, these experiences are not exclusive to monogamous people. Zachary is polyamorous and told me that in the past, when he dated someone who was a woman, his friends were incredibly dismissive of their relationship. Comments were normally said behind his back, he noted, but eventually he would find out. This experience was not uncommon for him and he stated that he often found his relationships were invalidated, especially when he was dating a cis woman, even if said woman was m-spec.

Zachary also recalled a past relationship with someone whose friends often made m-spec phobic comments to his ex. Zachary was unaware that his ex was often defending him to their friends as they said such things like, 'You don't want to date a bi man', as the friends believed Zachary was simply closeted and would eventually end up with a woman.

Ethical non-monogamy

Ethical non-monogamy is 'the umbrella term for practicing relationships that are not sexually and/or romantically exclusive' (Hy 2019), where ethical is stated to express the fact that there is enthusiastic consent from all parties involved in the relationship.

There are a number of different ways that ethical non-monogamy is practised. Open relationships are when one, or both, people within a couple 'engage in sexual/romantic relations outside the couple' (Hy 2019). Polyamory is often used when people engage in multiple relationships that include both a romantic and sexual aspect.

Ethical non-monogamy can look many different ways and it is up to the people involved to define the way that this is formed. A key part of this is communication, and ensuring that the rules and boundaries are set and adhered to. Of course, this holds for any form of relationship, including monogamous relationships.

According to Haupert *et al.* (2017), it was seen that approximately one in five people in the US have engaged in consensual non-monogamy at some point in their lives. Unfortunately, our society often gives non-monogamy a bad rap as monogamy is often deemed the only acceptable way to have a relationship.

People who are non-monogamous often have to deal with a number of misconceptions about them and their relationships. As discussed by Hope (2019), polyamorous and non-monogamous people are often seen to be cheaters or unsatisfied with their sex life with their partner. They are seen as sexually indiscriminate, as 'promiscuous', 'slutty' or 'sex-crazed', willing to have sex with anyone and everyone.

Of course, there is absolutely nothing wrong with being slutty or promiscuous. But society often looks down on people who are sexually liberated and misunderstands the fundamental ideas of what it means to be non-monogamous. These attributes are linked with dishonesty and depravity, rather than openness and freedom.

When m-spec identities are mixed in with this, the stigma attached can become far greater. The misconceptions are amplified and combined with m-spec phobia and erasure.

Bobby is a bisexual man married to a cis straight woman and they have semi-open non-monogamous relationship. She is currently not actively looking for any sort of relationship outside their marriage, although the option is available, while Bobby is allowed to explore outside their relationship with other men only. While there is that restriction on their openness, this doesn't matter to Bobby as his extra-marital interests lie with men.

He gives this information upfront when it comes to dating and hook-up apps and tends not to get any negative feedback but, when he does, it tends to be rooted in m-spec phobia. He often gets told that he is actually gay and it is only a matter of time until he comes out. His wife tends to garner sympathy as a result and he gets told that he is doing her a disservice. He also hears that he's greedy and is just using men, treating them like trash.

You can see here how all of these comments are both misunderstanding what bisexual and m-spec identities mean as well as what it means to be open and non-monogamous. While it was a difficult road for Bobby and his wife to understand each other and come to an arrangement to ensure their wants and desires were met, they are happily married and in love.

Bobby wanting to explore and express his sexuality outside his marriage doesn't mean he's doing his wife a disservice. If anything, it is the opposite. Having open communication and mutual consent and respect is a sign of a healthy and supportive relationship. And his desire for men doesn't make him gay, especially since he is happily married to a woman.

The struggle here is the way society paints monosexuality and monogamy as the norm. This is where a lot of the bigotry around both m-spec identities and non-monogamy comes from, where the norm is constantly reinforced and projected onto people who sit outside it. So when society looks at Bobby's situation, instead of recognizing a bisexual man married to a woman and in an open relationship, it sees a gay man married to a woman to hide his identity while cheating on her.

We can see this in the way 'greedy' is used to label both m-spec people and non-monogamous people. The norm is that people are attracted to one gender and enter a relationship with a single person. To want or desire anything beyond that is seen to be excessive, as more than the usual person needs and therefore greedy.

But there is nothing excessive about being attracted to more than one gender and nothing selfish about wanting to have relationships with more than one person. This doesn't make someone 'unsatisfiable', as it is often said. Attraction and desire present in many different forms, and fulfilling your desires is normal.

Coming out in a relationship

We have already discussed coming out and how incredibly difficult it can be as a process in general, but particularly for m-spec people. This can be even harder when in a relationship. What if you only come to terms with your identity while you're in a relationship? How do you inform your partner? Is it even necessary to do so?

There is, naturally, a fear that the relationship will fall apart as a result of coming out even if it fundamentally doesn't change anything in and of itself. Your attraction to your partner is unlikely to have changed and unless you are also wanting a change in your relationship dynamic in order to accommodate your exploration, everything is as it was. Opening up to your partner and sharing this potentially new-found part of yourself shouldn't be such a terrifying ordeal.

But it can easily go sour. In February 2020, Netflix aired a new show called *Love Is Blind*, a reality dating show with a bizarre concept. The show starts with a group of people who date each other, but the twist is they never see each other. After ten days of this, the men are able to propose to the woman they want to marry. Only then can they see what the person they've been talking to looks like.

They then spend time in a retreat with all the couples and get to know one another, eventually going to an apartment and meeting each other's family before the big day. On the wedding day itself, they get the final question, 'Is love blind?' and decide whether to split up or get married.

On the show, one of the couples was Carlton and Diamond. Dating had gone well and Diamond accepted Carlton's proposal. However, their relationship imploded at the resort when Carlton disclosed his sexuality. He informed Diamond about his relationship history, that he had been with both men and women, and loved people at their core not their gender. Bisexual was used to describe Carlton.

This threw Diamond, who was visibly shocked, and caused her to have doubts about their relationship. A partner disclosing their sexuality as something other than your assumption, usually straight when in the context of different sex relationships, can be a lot to process and Diamond stated this before going back to her room for the night.

However, the next day, the conversation took a left turn. Diamond accused Carlton of playing the experiment, of being dishonest and withholding information. She said he should have stated his sexuality upfront, so she could have made a better decision, and made it clear that he wanted to be with a female. She injected doubt into his feelings, stating that he had led her to believe he really had feelings for her.

Carlton's reaction to this was awful, to say the least. He started lashing out, he shut down, became rude and aggressive and cursed at her. His behaviour was completely unacceptable and the conversation could have been handled a lot better.

It was clear from this conversation that Diamond did not understand what bisexuality, or being m-spec, actually meant. Her comments were clearly rooted in ignorance and m-spec phobia, not understanding the issues m-spec men face and why they might potentially hide their identity. She didn't seem to understand that his sexuality didn't change his feelings for her, or meant that he had picked a gender, and that in fact it fundamentally changed nothing about their relationship.

Unfortunately, Diamond's reaction is not uncommon. Coming out as m-spec often leads to being bombarded with comments rooted in bigotry. Part of coming out to anyone, especially those you care about, does means being prepared to answer those questions and help people understand your sexuality and, by extension, you. It becomes a teachable moment.

But should this burden always fall on us? These questions aren't always easy to answer and the concepts can be difficult to explain, especially when you are under the stress of coming out or barely understanding your own relationship with your identity. It is hoped that, if the person truly loves you, they will put in the work to learn and understand your sexuality and unlearn their bigotry.

James P told me of his experience of coming out to his wife. He had held attraction towards multiple genders from a young age, but had never heard of any m-spec identities before. Due to the binary construction of sexuality in his mind, he found himself going back and forth between gay and straight. He used his attraction towards women as a way to label his feelings towards men as nothing more than a phase, denying that attraction.

Eventually he fell in love with a woman, settled down, got married and had kids. His sexuality may seem irrelevant at this point, but of course he was hiding a part of himself which was causing undue harm internally. He told me how he felt as if he had to self-censor his words and behaviour to keep up the image that he was straight, and how exhausting this could be.

Coming out to his wife was a moment filled with fear for James P; fear that the relationship would implode terrified him. Of course, if he was gay, the fall-out would still be painful but would mean he could move forward to a better life. But James P wasn't seeking anything more from his life. He was content in his marriage and loved his family, and he didn't want anything to change. He said that coming out felt like throwing a grenade into his happy life, destroying everything he held dear for nothing.

But it was not necessarily for nothing. His mental state wasn't great and hiding this part of himself was making him miserable. He wanted to be himself. James P being bisexual didn't change his attraction to his wife, his relationship or anything that they have built together, but it did allow James P to be open about himself and embrace his identity.

Bobby not only came out as bisexual but expressed his desire for a change in his relationship dynamic to his wife. While she responded positively to Bobby being bisexual at first, she struggled with his desires and needs. Coming out as non-monogamous a few years later added strain to their relationship. His love for her and a desire to be with her had not changed, but he no longer wished to be in a monogamous relationship and wanted to explore his sexuality and have sexual relations with men.

This nearly spelled the end for their relationship as his wife desired a monogamous relationship and their journey was incredibly difficult, but eventually they reached a place of mutual understanding and were able to move forward. They went through a lot of pain and heartache but now have a happy and healthy marriage where both of their desires and needs are met and Bobby is supported in his exploration.

Coming out to your partner can be a difficult experience. It is a moment filled with anxiety and dread, fear for what might happen to your relationship, even if your love for the other person has not changed.

For Javier Vilalta, however, coming out as bisexual to his ex-wife resulted in him being sued. Vilalta, who lives in Spain, had been in a relationship with his wife from the age of 16 to 34, was married for three of those years and divorced in 2009 (Garrido 2020; Maurice 2020). He identified as straight while he was in a relationship with her. After divorcing his wife, he had doubts about his personality which prompted him to get therapy, where he was able to discover that he was bisexual. He told his ex-wife this in 2016, as he was still on good terms with her.

However, in 2019, some of his and his ex-wife's mutual friends assured her that he was, and is, gay as he had had relationships with men before they married and since their divorce. This prompted her to file a lawsuit against Vilalta. She said that, had she known this information, she never would have married him. She accused him of concealing his homosexuality and using her to hide his sexuality, suing him for €10,000 for economic and moral damages and demanding an annulment of their union.

Vilalta's lawyer argued that Vilalta had never misled his wife and the fact that he was bisexual did not mean he couldn't have a relationship with a woman. However, the judge ruled against him and ordered Vilalta to pay €3000 to his ex-wife, €1000 for each year they had been married. Neither in the lawsuit nor in the sentence is Vilalta's actual sexuality – bisexual – ever acknowledged. He is completely erased as bisexual, portrayed as homosexual and penalized for this.

This highlights the issue m-spec men face when coming out in a relationship. While not everyone will be sued, this may not be an isolated incident. M-spec identities are not acknowledged and are actively erased, not just by individuals but on a structural level. Vilalta's identity was erased, not just by his supposed friends, not just by his ex-wife with whom he'd had a good relationship until that point, but by the entire judicial system.

It is upsetting and frustrating that the court demanded Vilalta pay damages to his wife for the sheer fact that he wasn't solely attracted to women. Worse than this, this could easily set a precedence in the courts, which can make it even harder for people to come out. Instead of being shown sympathy for the difficulty in realizing and revealing your identity, it can be thrown back at you, and you could be forced to pay damages to those you were previously in relationships with.

This ruling revokes a person's right to privacy, as they are unable to conceal their identity if they wish to do so for fear of repercussion in the future. It also entirely dismisses the fact that sexuality can grow and change as people gain new knowledge and have new experiences.

Positive experiences

So, while dating and relationships can be harder for m-spec men, they aren't impossible. As we can see, there are plenty of out and proud m-spec men who are dating successfully or in relationships, living their best lives and forming deep bonds with people.

I haven't had much success when it comes to dating myself, but I am currently in a relationship with a cisallo gay man. While I am normally quite upfront about my sexuality, I met my current partner on an app and failed to realize that my sexuality was not on my profile until after we had started chatting. I mentioned it offhandedly during a conversation and it was completely unquestioned. Not only is my sexuality not seen as an obstacle in any way, I find that it is supported and loved.

While Bobby had a bumpy road coming out to his wife as bisexual and non-monogamous, he now finds himself in a happy marriage with the freedom to explore his sexuality. He has rare moments of negativity on the apps, but often finds people who are not so concerned with his sexuality or relationship status. However, he does tend to seek out people who are already partnered, which is both his wife's and his preference, as he isn't interested in having a romantic relationship outside his marriage.

Zachary told me how he moved to New York specifically to cultivate the life he desired. He found sanctum in sex clubs, which he has found to be incredibly welcoming and progressive spaces. His bisexuality and polyamory are very welcomed there and he can have the adventurous experiences he desires and build bonds with like-minded people.

Zachary also told me how he tends to date other m-spec people as well as people who are non-binary, genderfluid or gender non-conforming, and experiences little to no m-spec phobia or erasure among these groups of people.

Advice

So what do m-spec men recommend when it comes to dating and relationships? How do you approach the dating scene and enter relationships? And how do you approach the conversation of your sexuality when it comes to this part of your life? And are there any barriers m-spec men have in this regard?

Terrence stressed the importance of finding what you are comfortable with. He recommended exploring your sexuality with as many people of as many different genders as you are comfortable with. This can help you figure out your sexuality, but it is important to be honest about what you want from the encounter. He also mentioned to not let society define your label for you or put you in a box and make you live up to certain expectations.

Zachary highly recommended that people be upfront about their sexuality, and many others agreed with this. Of course, this can be tricky, as Terrence said. Telling someone your sexuality isn't always easy and you need to make sure you are comfortable sharing that part of yourself with someone. Terrence told me how if he is with a straight woman, he may not mention his sexuality until the second date.

This also isn't achievable for everyone. If you aren't fully out and are concerned someone may find out, it's natural to want to hide your sexuality. For some, it may be the fear that stating your sexuality upfront may lead to reduced opportunities. But Alex said that if you aren't closeted, he recommended putting your sexuality on your bio on dating apps and telling people upfront.

Being upfront may appear to reduce your desirability and limit your opportunities, but most of the people I spoke to agreed that this is for the best. At the end of the day, the last thing you want to do is date someone only to discover they are m-spec phobic. Alex said that stating it upfront helps you weed out these people and may even lessen the number of negative experiences you have. Zachary added that being upfront with your sexuality will open the door to other m-spec people and increase your opportunities there.

For those who are closeted, Alex recommended going to m-spec-specific events and, if you are polyamorous, specific events that cater to that. These spaces can help you find like-minded people and express yourself more freely, with less fear of having to come out or experience bigotry.

Of course, these spaces aren't always easy to find and it may be harder if you live outside a major city. Finding other m-spec people in general can even be difficult, due to the low coming out rates. But having spaces which aren't so gay orientated or dominated can be wonderful, not just for closeted people but for all m-spec people, regardless of whether you are trying to find people to date.

For those who are struggling with dating and experiencing m-spec phobia or erasure, these spaces can help remove that issue. Zachary highly recommended this, saying that finding and dating other m-spec people can be such a blessing. It often means not having to explain a lot of the difficulties you face, since you have that shared experience. And it means you can relate to each other on that. He did, however, stress the importance of not bonding solely over this trauma as that can be unhealthy.

Some people stated that they hold certain preferences when it comes to dating. Several people noted that while they didn't rule out cisallo straight women, they did tend to avoid them and favour queer women. This is either due to past experiences of dealing with m-spec phobia, the expectation from that sort of relationship or the fear of being in a heteronormative dynamic. A few also noted that they tend to favour other m-spec people, as it removed the stigma entirely.

In terms of coming out when you're already in a relationship, Bobby said that being open about your sexuality is the best thing you can do for your mental health. It is important to consider what you want in terms of coming out. Do you desire a change in your relationship dynamic or do you simply want to share this part of yourself? There is, naturally, the risk of things falling apart but living your truth is important. Your sexuality is a part of you, and it is important to be with someone who loves the entirety of you.

Relationships are always difficult and always require work, but a strong relationship should be built on a foundation of communication and trust. James P agreed with this. Even though he desired no change in his relationship, he wanted to share this part of himself with his wife as it is important to be open and authentic in a relationship.

Of course, coming out is always a personal choice and you should only ever do so when you feel ready. Remember, you don't owe anyone this information. You do not have to come out to anyone unless you want to and feel safe and comfortable sharing that part of yourself.

Trusting your partner and expressing your identity can be incredibly important and coming out to them can lift a heavy burden. It can also help so many other people. Visibility, as already mentioned, is incredibly important. Hiding yourself when in a monogamous relationship buys into the idea that m-spec people eventually choose a side, and it reduces visibility. Your sexuality is a beautiful part of you, so be sure to embrace and celebrate it.

CHAPTER 4

Health

According to Stonewall, 59 per cent of bi people reported experiencing depression compared to 46 per cent of gay/lesbian people (2020); 56 per cent of bi men experienced anxiety compared to 53 per cent of gay men (2018); 18 per cent of bi men had self-harmed versus 7 per cent of gay men (2018); and 43 per cent of bi men had suicidal ideation versus 32 per cent of gay men (2018). While it is never a good idea to play Oppression Olympics – fighting for who is the most oppressed and who has it worse – it's important to note the discrepancies between different groups within the LGBTQIA + community and analyse the root cause.

In this case, these discrepancies between m-spec men and gay men are likely borne out of m-spec phobia and erasure, which m-spec men have to deal with on top of the same homophobia that gay men have to deal with. We experience double discrimination, where both the cisallo straight community and the LGBTQIA+ community refuse to accept us within their space. M-spec men are so often erased, told they are gay and discriminated against on that basis.

These statistics can be seen outside the UK too. According to the *Invisible Majority* report (Movement Advancement Project 2016), while men who identified as gay had higher rates of mood and anxiety disorders than those men who identified as bisexual, men who had sex with both men and women (regardless of how they identified) were markedly higher for both mood and anxiety disorders than any other men. Numerous other studies appear to corroborate this finding, as seen in Rainbow Health Ontario's (n.d.) fact sheet.

And it is not just mental health where m-spec men struggle. As mentioned in a previous chapter, there is a stigma attached to m-spec men when it comes to sexual health. M-spec men are painted as disease spreaders who are responsible for bringing HIV from the gay community to straight people. This stigma could be preventing m-spec men from accessing sexual health resources. Is enough work being done to reach m-spec men to help with their sexual health and tackle the stigma surrounding them?

As we have already seen, m-spec men are often reluctant to come out. The same trend can be seen in regard to healthcare. In 2020, according to Stonewall, 40 per cent of bi men weren't out to anyone when seeking medical care, compared to just 10 per cent of gay men; 21 per cent of bi people stated that healthcare professionals didn't understand their specific health needs; and 22 per cent said they experienced inappropriate curiosity from healthcare professionals (Stonewall 2020).

When looking specifically at bi men, it was seen that 17 per cent experienced inappropriate curiosity (on a par with gay men) and 15 per cent experienced a lack of understanding (Stonewall 2018). The latter was less than the figure for gay men, which stood at 19 per cent; however, this may be due to bi men being less likely to disclose in an effort to avoid this issue.

M-spec men's health is clearly impacted by the m-spec phobia and erasure that are prevalent in our society. Not only does this detrimentally impact their mental health and create a negative image of their sexual health, it also creates barriers for them in terms of accessing the support and resources they need to overcome these challenges.

How can m-spec men fight their depression or anxiety if they experience discrimination from the very care that is supposed to support them? Are there resources available that specifically target and cater to m-spec men? In this chapter, we will be delving into the experiences of m-spec men in regards to their mental health and sexual health and how they overcame the barriers that they faced.

Mental Health

The statistics from numerous different sources show, quite clearly, that m-spec men have higher rates of depression, anxiety, self-harm and suicidal ideation than gay men. The information and stories that we have seen so far make the reason for this disparity quite clear. M-spec phobia and erasure impact every part of m-spec people's lives, from school to the workplace, their family bonds and relationships. On top of this, m-spec men also often experience homophobia, just like gay men.

All of this prevents m-spec men from understanding who they are, makes them fearful of coming out and creates constant doubt about their sexuality. It becomes even more difficult when the community that is supposed to support them also discriminates against them, cutting them off from spaces, meaning they're without the networks that could help them. This will be unpacked more in a later chapter, but we have already seen examples of this.

Naturally, this all has an impact on the mental wellbeing of m-spec men. I spoke to numerous m-spec men who all told me about how their confusion over their sexuality, being closeted or denying their feelings impacted their mental state.

Issues with mental health

Y is one such person. While Y was trying to accept his identity as a bisexual, demisexual man, he often found himself confused over his identity. But learning to accept his own identity was only one step, he told me, while expressing fear over the idea of being pushed away were he to ever express his bisexuality to a close friend. This may relate to the way he was treated growing up, being made to feel unmanly due to his interest in things considered 'feminine' in his culture. As a result of his struggle with his identity, Y continues to experience depression and social anxiety.

This is something that I too can relate to, as mentioned previously. There is that expectation to be masculine, as expressing femininity is often seen as indicative of being gay. I often found myself berated for my supposed femininity and lack of masculinity. I felt for a long time that I was broken, wrong. This meant I suffered from depression for a long time – although I didn't realise at the time that it was in fact depression – as well as anxiety and suicidal ideation.

I often wished that I could end my life, but I never attempted suicide. Instead, I found myself praying for an event to occur that would bring my life to an end.

Gordon suffers from chronic moderate to severe anxiety and depression due to remaining closeted for decades. While there were other issues at play, this caused quite a big impact on his mental state. Despite knowing his sexuality when he was a teenager, he only came out publicly at 54.

Stigma surrounding mental health

Mental wellbeing is incredibly important, so if you are experiencing issues with your mental health, it is vital to get help. However, there are a lot of issues when it comes to getting help, such as stigma, access to and availability of resources, quality care and more. Due to the stigma surrounding mental health some people decide not to access support services despite the fact that they are struggling. Gordon told me that he didn't access mental health services until he was in his 30s. This is due to the fact that he was raised with the idea that going to therapy meant that you were weak, needy or incapable. The stigma around therapy meant he didn't get help despite struggling with depression and anxiety for some time, which was partly caused by being closeted.

Not only does this stigma mean that you may not access mental health services when you need it, which can cause your condition to deteriorate, but the stigma itself can exacerbate the issue. Statistics from the Mental Health Foundation (n.d.) show that nearly 90 per cent of people who have mental health issues reported that stigma had a negative effect on their lives and it was noted that many people's problems are made worse by the stigma.

For example, if you are struggling with depression or low mood, you may already have feelings of being a failure. Therefore it stands to reason that the stigma around mental health, which tells you that needing support makes you a less worthy or less

HEALTH

valuable person, like Gordon experienced, will exacerbate this
issue and worsen your depression.

The American Psychiatry Association (n.d.) noted several
issues around mental health stigma, such as reduced hope
and self-esteem, increased difficulties at work and worsening
symptoms. It also noted that not only are people more reluctant
to seek treatment, but there is a reduced likelihood that they
will stick with treatment when they do access it, and therefore
they have a poorer recovery.

The concept of masculinity also plays a huge part in the
stigma surrounding discussing mental health issues for men.
What makes someone masculine or feminine is borne out of
traditional gender roles which are archaic, toxic and incredibly
stifling. Men are expected to be the providers, to be strong and
successful, while women are expected to be caregivers, to be
nurturing, emotional and weak. As mentioned in the chapter
on coming out, men are often punished for transgressing from
masculinity and these expectations and, as a result, they often
avoid anything that may be perceived as feminine.

There is an added social pressure for men when it comes to
discussing their mental health. Talking about your emotions
and issues is seen as a womanly trait, as feminine, and therefore unmasculine. Men are berated when they talk about their
emotions and, as a result, can often bottle up their problems,
which only causes their issues to worsen. This is often known
as toxic masculinity.

Toxic masculinity is where the expectations of masculinity
and what it means to be a man negatively impact the society
in which men live, as well as themselves. It is often one of the
root causes behind the misogynistic abuse that women face
and queerphobia that LGBTQIA+ people deal with. As well as

harming others, toxic masculinity can also hurt men themselves, preventing them from being able to do certain things or hold certain characteristics.

Chatmon (2020) discuss toxic masculinity and its role in the mental health stigma that men experience as well as the impact this has on the wellbeing of men. In this article, Chatmon says that toxic masculinity results in men struggling to express their emotions, and adherence to these norms can lead to worse mental health outcomes. It is noted that 'depression and suicide are ranked as a leading cause of death among men' and that men are 'far less likely to seek mental health treatment than women' (p.1).

I should note here that this structure is created by men. The society in which we live is patriarchal, it is controlled by men. It is men who have constructed the idea that men are strong and powerful, while women are weak. And this stigma, this pressure to adhere to masculinity, is borne out of misogyny. To display feminine traits is to be like a woman, a weaker and lesser being in our patriarchal society. This is undesirable for men, so they force themselves to adhere to masculine norms so as to not face abuse.

While some women and people of other genders may uphold this system, expect or demand men to be masculine and a 'real' man, it is men who are responsible for creating this system and continually upholding it. It is men who are the biggest perpetrators in berating other men who stray away from these ideals. Men have created a system that not only harms others, such as women through misogyny, but also themselves.

As discussed previously, I often found myself berated by my dad and male peers for showing any feminine traits. I was told off for crying and told to 'stop acting like a girl'. I personally didn't feel comfortable in expressing my emotions fully and the issues I was going through as I knew I would be told to 'stop being dramatic' and 'man up'. Blizzb3ar experienced similar issues. He told me that he wasn't able to access resources as getting help for mental health often made you appear weak and less masculine. As a result, he found that he had to put on a facade of emotional stability.

There are other aspects besides stigma that could be at play when it comes to barriers people face in taking that first step and seeking help. For example, Blizzb3ar said that he was often told to pray away his issues. I was often told that my issues 'weren't that bad' and to be thankful for all that I have. Pressures from family, friends and community can often be contributing factors in dissuading people from accessing the help they so desperately need.

Accessing and availability of services

The desire to access mental health services is just the first hurdle. The next is having the means or services available to you.

In the UK, some mental health services are free on the NHS, but waiting lists can be incredibly long. This can make it difficult to get help as and when you need it. *The Independent* saw in 2019 that the Improving Access to Psychological Therapies (IAPT) scheme was often rushing people through the system to give them their first appointment so targets could be met, only to make them endure long waits for a follow-up appointment (Gregory 2019).

In the US, accessing therapy entirely depends on the insurance you have and some may not cover it, meaning you will have to pay yourself. Paying for therapy can become costly, as you may need regular sessions over a prolonged period of time for it to really have any impact.

Data from Healthline (Fraga 2021) shows that therapy can cost between $65 and $150 per session, and upwards of $200 in expensive cities. With most people needing five to ten sessions, therapy without insurance would cost $325 total at the very minimum, which is not an expense everyone can afford.

In the UK, multiple people spoke to me about their struggles to get an appointment on the NHS and the huge waiting times they experienced. James P mentioned that he only waited a few weeks for the initial screening appointment but was then made to wait for around three months before he had his first actual session with a therapist. This is similar to what I experienced myself and showcases what we previously mentioned.

R spoke to his GP about the issues he was experiencing but found that the waiting time for an appointment with a mental health professional on the NHS was excessive, and the same was seen for the university's wellbeing service. This discouraged him from seeking the help he needed.

Terence had one of the worst waiting times. After being referred by a clinic in East London to a counsellor at a charity that provided mental health support in partnership with the NHS trust, he was made to wait 18 months before finally receiving the support he needed.

These waiting times mean that people inevitably suffer and their condition deteriorates. It was reported in *The Guardian* (Bawden, Campbell and Duncan 2018) that 'at least 271 highly vulnerable mental health patients' died between 2012 and 2017 due to failures in NHS care. These included early discharge without adequate support, poor or inappropriate care and delayed treatment.

Hann is from the US and suffers from depression, which they said was worsened due to their sexual orientation, living with a constant fear that their bisexuality was just a phase. He was lucky enough to gain access to therapy under his parents' insurance growing up; however, under the Affordable Care Act (aka Obamacare) he lost access to this when he turned 26. Since then, Hann has found it incredibly difficult to access therapy.

As they are based in Massachusetts and earn below the poverty line, they are automatically enrolled in MassHealth insurance, but struggled to find a competent professional who would take it. They told me that even if they had excellent insurance, a lot of therapists don't take it and require you to pay. This is not a viable option for Hann.

This is not an issue Hann faces alone. According to The Williams Institute (Badgett, Durso and Schneebaum 2013), in the US, 25.9 per cent of bisexual men live at or below the poverty level. This is compared to 20.5 per cent of gay men and 15.3 per cent of straight men. The poverty rate for the US as a whole in 2011 was 15 per cent.

So you can see how bisexual and m-spec men are more likely to live at or below the poverty level. With the lack of free healthcare in the US and many mental health professionals refusing to take free state-based insurance as Hann mentioned, it means that m-spec men are unable to get access to the help that they so desperately need.

Worse than this, data from KFF (n.d.) shows that numerous states have a huge lack of mental health provision, such as Missouri, where only 5.9 per cent of the need is met. CNBC noted that 'more than 112 million Americans live in areas where mental health providers are scarce' (Leonhardt 2021).

They also mention that only '56% of psychiatrists accept commercial insurance compared to 90% of other, non-mental health physicians' and that this was due to insurers demanding more paperwork and paying lower rates to mental health professionals (Leonhardt 2021).

Quality of care

The stigma around mental health is likely to be the first hurdle people have to overcome. They have to push past this in order to reach out and get the help they need. The next hurdle is the waiting lists or costs associated with mental health. Long waiting lists or care that is outside people's budget can shut people out of getting the help they need when they need it. This can cause their condition to worsen or even prove fatal.

The next barrier is getting effective and quality care. As we have already noted, m-spec men have trouble with healthcare professionals. M-spec men are more likely to encounter staff who do not understand their identity or their needs and are more likely than gay men to be made uncomfortable due to inappropriate questions. The fear of this experience forces m-spec men to avoid disclosing their identity altogether. This means that even if you are able to gain access to therapy, as an m-spec man you may not be able to get the help you require for the problems you are experiencing. In fact, your problems may only worsen.

In *Women in Relationships with Bisexual Men: Bi Men By Women*, Pallotta-Chiarolli (2016), as the title suggests, works with women of varying sexualities who happen to be in a relationship with bisexual men.

Of particular interest, at least for this chapter, is Chapter 16 of Pallotta-Chiarolli's book, which discusses the misrepresentation and erasure of bisexuality in health services. One contributor, Heather, spoke to her doctor about 'the mental health ramifications of her partner's bisexuality'; she found that her doctor was 'blown away. Her little head was spinning and she didn't really know what to say' (p.441).

I think it's important to note here that I do believe in the importance of centring the experiences of bisexual and m-spec men and the issues and struggles they face, rather than those of their partners. It doesn't sit entirely right with me to read about the mental health issues that this woman has experienced due to her partner being bisexual and focusing on that rather than the mental health issues these bisexual men have faced themselves.

However, this book does provide some truly fascinating insights on how m-spec identities are perceived and does cover the issues bisexual and m-spec men face, even if it does centre on women's experiences in relation to this. The reasoning for Pallotta-Chiarolli's focus on the women in these relationships rather than the m-spec men themselves may be due to the structures at play. Would Pallotta-Chiarolli have been given the opportunity, the funding, the publishing offer, if she didn't at least appear to be focusing on cisallohet women? This is something I discuss more deeply in the sexual health chapter.

What this extract shows is that there is a lack of knowledge of m-spec identities and the issues surrounding them among healthcare professionals. This is backed up by the experiences of m-spec men I spoke to.

The last therapist that Hann had didn't discriminate against him, and in fact Hann found them to be very open and understanding. However, they did find that this therapist was completely clueless on LGBTQIA+ issues. This meant that Hann ended up having to teach their own therapist, explaining a lot of the issues they were facing. How can m-spec men expect therapists to help them with their issues when they don't understand the problems they are experiencing?

James P had a very similar experience to Hann. He found that his therapist didn't understand what it meant to be bisexual and closeted, asking why it mattered to James P to come out since he was already with the one he loved and that everyone has secrets.

His therapist likened it to how people wear different masks with different people, how they see different sides of us.

James P tried to explain further to his therapist why it was an issue and, using his therapist's own analogy, explained how he felt as if he was constantly in a play, wearing a mask, performing an act that he could never drop. He explained how exhausting this was, but his therapist didn't understand it.

Ismail spent a few days in a mental institution after his issues spiralled out of control and he was grappling with suicidal ideation. During his time there, he was asked by one of the doctors about his masturbation patterns and whether he masturbated to both gay and straight porn. When Ismail answered yes, the doctor responded that Ismail was bisexual. The fact that a mental health professional couldn't take Ismail's word on his identity and, worse than that, thought that the porn someone masturbates to is what determines their identity, shows the bigoted views that exist among some healthcare professionals.

Pathologization of m-spec identities

Unfortunately, this is how sexuality is often examined by those working in scientific fields. In 2020, a study was published entitled 'Robust evidence for bisexual orientation among men', which collected data from various historic studies that examined the arousal patterns of self-identified bisexual men (Bailey et al. 2020). The studies involved heterosexual, homosexual and bisexual identifying men being made to watch pornography and having their penile circumference measured and compared to a baseline to indicate whether they were aroused or not. This pornography would vary between showing male or female sexual acts (either masturbating or same-sex encounters). While not made clear, I think it is safe to assume that these studies were binary in nature. From the men included to the sexual acts they were shown, trans and non-binary people were likely excluded.

By examining the arousal of these men from different stimuli, the researchers were able to see whether the arousal patterns were in line with what they expected from the men based on their sexual orientation. With this study, which collected data from various others who carried out this investigation, they were able to conclude that bisexuality in men existed, as the data showed this.

The studies were conducted by psychologists and published in a scientific journal. Why was this necessary? Why do these psychologists think it necessary to examine genital arousal in order to confirm that bisexual and m-spec men exist? Why are they incapable of simply believing that these men are what they say they are?

It's troubling to see that psychologists may believe that arousal to porn indicates your identity. It is missing so much of what makes someone's identity and their attraction to others. Personality, romance, intimacy and so much more can make up part of someone's attraction to people, and removing all of that is crude and dehumanizing. Even on a sexual level, there is so much that can make someone sexually attracted to another person beyond the audio/visual that pornography provides.

The fact that psychologists and mental health professionals, as seen with Ismail, can boil down your sexuality to arousal to pornography and think you need to prove your identity is concerning. What does this say about the care that m-spec men may receive? Will the care be of a good quality when these are the views and ideas held by healthcare professionals? What does this say about the education being provided to those who may one day be entrusted with our mental health issues?

In 'Mental health services experiences of bisexual women and bisexual men', Page (2004) looked at the experiences that bisexual people had when accessing mental health services. They saw that a number of people found their sexuality 'invalidated and pathologized' either because the clinician 'assumed that the client's bisexuality was connected to clinical issues when the client didn't agree' or 'assumed that bisexual attractions and behavior would disappear when the client regained psychological health' (p.147).

It is important to state that the issues m-spec people face are not because they are m-spec. Being m-spec isn't a sign of mental health issues, and our sexuality won't change after getting the help we need. The mental health issues are due to our experiences, our struggles. They are due to the structural monosexism that results in the erasure and bigotry that m-spec people face.

And it's important to remember that. These experiences stop us from coming out, force us to hide our identity, and mean we are constantly invalidated when we do reveal our identity. They make dating and relationships harder to obtain. This all has an impact on our mental wellbeing.

The pathologizing of m-spec identities means that mental health professionals refuse to believe that m-spec identities are normal, that they exist, and so they invalidate their client's identity. This means that m-spec people are who are seeking the help they need are often subjected to further discrimination, which may put them off accessing help. This creates a new barrier for m-spec people, who may continue to suffer with their mental health issues as they are unable to get the support they need.

In *Women in Relationships with Bisexual Men: Bi Men By Women* (Pallotta-Chiarolli 2016), there are numerous instances where the women or their partner, the bisexual man, sought help from a therapist or other medical professional, such as their GP, only to be met with discrimination – from some men being told that their relationship would die, to others being convinced that they were gay and should leave their wife. It is clear that these healthcare professionals didn't see m-spec identities as valid.

In several instances, these professionals were gay men and projected their own experience onto their client. One of the women, Rachel, mentioned how a gay doctor both herself and her husband were seeing clearly had an agenda to split them up. The doctor told her that she 'needed to get help for my problem which was not being able to release my gay husband' (Pallotta-Chiarolli 2016, p.446). Another, Scarlett, said that her GP told her how he was in a similar situation and had left his wife, and it appeared that he was convincing her husband to leave her.

Intersectionality

The situation can worsen for those who are not just m-spec, but hold other identities at the same time. Ismail struggled with both obsessive compulsive disorder (OCD) and anxiety prior to questioning his identity but found his condition was exacerbated by his sexual identity. When he sought help, his therapist was completely clueless on matters of race and dismissed his experiences.

CJ found that after an attempted suicide and forced hospitalization, he was treated horrifically by mental health professionals who misgendered him and blamed his issues on the fact that he was trans.

I will be talking more on the issues experienced by those who belong to more than one marginalized group in a later chapter but it's important to mention here how this creates yet another barrier to accessing the help and support m-spec men need.

Getting help

While there are clearly many issues around m-spec men getting the care they need, and some have experiences that are far from ideal, a number of m-spec men told me how much these services have helped them.

James P may have had to wait a few months to get help on the NHS only to deal with a therapist who was clueless on the struggle of being bisexual and closeted, but he found the process useful nonetheless. Therapy helped James P to process his thoughts and his journey so far in life; it enabled him to get his head straight and talk openly about himself and what he was struggling with. It made a huge difference to his life, changing his mood, and gave him the courage to open up to his wife.

Terence had to wait an extremely long time to get the help he needed but found it very useful when he finally did get it. His counsellor helped him to accept himself, affirmed the difficulties bisexual and m-spec men face and told him he had a right to be what he was. It helped expand his vocabulary so that he could fully articulate his feelings about his experiences as well as what he wanted and needed going forward. This whole process was incredibly beneficial to Terence and his mental health.

Jay purposely sought out a queer-friendly therapist. MyMind in Ireland allowed him to filter therapists based on who was knowledgeable on LGBTQIA+ issues, so he was able to find a therapist who understood his issues. He found this space incredibly useful as it gave him the opportunity to be open and honest about his issues and it has helped him to come out to more and more people.

VR has had a similar experience with Open Path Collective, allowing him to find affordable mental healthcare in New York City with people who were queer and very well educated on the issues LGBTQIA+ people face, which allowed him to work on his struggles with depression and anxiety. Pink Therapy is similar to MyMind and Open Path Collective, allowing you to find LGBTQIA+ specialized therapists in the UK and get the help you need.

There are also a number of charities which provide free therapy, peer support, group therapy or helplines and work directly with LGBTQIA+ people. LGBT Foundation, LGBT Switchboard and MindOut are three such examples of where people can go to access help in the UK and get more inclusive support than they otherwise would on the NHS. The Bi Survivors Network is an m-spec-specific organization that helps m-spec people who have experienced sexual and domestic violence, through bi-weekly virtual chats.

So, while it is clear that accessing help for your mental health is not easy, it is very important to do so. Accessing help means navigating a minefield of issues, from stigma to cost and further discrimination. But there are options available out there and it can make all the difference in improving your mental wellbeing.

Sexual Health

As we discussed in Chapter 1, the AIDS epidemic created an image that m-spec men are vectors for disease. They were painted as villains who bridge the gap between the homosexual and heterosexual communities causing HIV, a disease seen to only impact homosexual men and men who have had sex with men, to spread to unsuspecting and 'pure' heterosexual women and even their unborn babies.

The stigma around HIV and sexual health melded with monosexism and m-spec phobic narratives to create a perfect storm that caused direct harm to m-spec men, forcing many to go back in the closet or conceal their identity in order to reduce the discrimination they received.

The issues from this period persist to this day. Many m-spec men still conceal their identity for various reasons, even from medical professionals, and m-spec men are still seen by many to have HIV simply by virtue of their identity. This means that m-spec men may not be able to access the resources they need in order to protect themselves and look after their sexual health, which directly puts them at risk.

In this section, I will be discussing the topic of sexual health and m-spec men, the issues that they face and the impact it can cause.

Staying in the closet

As mentioned in Chapter 2 on coming out, Todd, a bisexual man I spoke to, decided to remain closeted during the AIDS epidemic. He told me that while his decision to be closeted was not initiated by the AIDS crisis, it was definitely reinforced by it. He first started having feelings for multiple genders around 11, which was five years before the first report of the AIDS crisis making national headlines.

His parents, like many others, associated AIDS with being gay. Naturally, m-spec identities weren't well known and were readily erased as they often tend to be, even in the present day, therefore any man who was attracted to or having sex with other men was seen to be gay. AIDS was also seen as a death sentence. Todd feared that if he came out, he would not only lose his parents' love but also burden his parents with the belief that eventually he would die from an AIDS-related illness.

In the book *Dual Attraction: Understanding Bisexuality* (Pryor,

Weinberg and Williams 1994), the authors interviewed various bisexual people between 1983 and 1988, to see how their lives changed. During this time, the AIDS crisis unfolded and we can see the direct impact this had on bisexual and m-spec people's lives.

The book reveals that the AIDS crisis altered the behaviours of these bisexual people and affected their relationships. It was noted that 40 per cent of their respondents mentioned becoming more wary of disclosing their bisexual identity, and 'three times as many men as women cited AIDS as a reason for becoming more wary' (p.274).

Some men mentioned only engaging in relationships with same-sex partners as relations with the heterosexual world worsened as bisexual men were painted as disease carriers. In fact, the number of men with no female partners rose from 4 per cent to 20 per cent and the number of men with five or more female partners fell from 33 per cent to 14 per cent.

A number of bisexual women in this book mentioned sex with men, especially bisexual men, as being more risky and therefore they became more interested in pursuing same-sex relationships and encounters. Some bisexual men mentioned that being seen as an AIDS risk caused their relationships with women to end, made it harder to find female partners and made them less comfortable in putting themselves out to women.

A number of bisexual men said they no longer had same-sex relationships. The number of men with no male partners rose from 14 per cent to around 33 per cent and the proportion who had five or more male partners fell from around 50 per cent to around 33 per cent.

AIDS was cited frequently by bisexual men, especially those who had tested negative, as they feared they would catch HIV. Some mentioned that it was harder to find male partners as spaces like bathhouses, often heavily populated with gay and bisexual men, were now empty. This, again, was likely due to the fear of AIDS causing people to retreat from these spaces and from sexual encounters with strangers in general.

There was also a fear not only of catching HIV themselves but passing it on to their female partners. Some of these men used their relationship with their girlfriend or wife to hide their identity and assume a straight label for themselves.

Throughout *Dual Attraction*, what can be seen is that while some bisexual men chose to retain their label and identity, their behaviours likely changed. Others decided to essentially submerge themselves in either the gay or straight communities and hide their bisexuality.

The bisexual bridge theory

The concept of the bisexual bridge theory clearly had a marked impact on the lives of these m-spec men, but how much of it is true? A study in San Francisco from 1994 entitled 'Are bisexually identified men in San Francisco a common vector for spreading HIV infection to women?' looked at the behaviours of bisexual men during the AIDS crisis and how these changed (Coates *et al.* 1994).

The study revealed huge drops in people who were having unprotected anal sex with multiple male partners, from 70 per cent to 12 per cent. The decline in unprotected sex was across the board, including those having unprotected anal sex with men and unprotected vaginal sex with women. These drops were more pronounced in those who were knowingly HIV positive.

It also showed a decrease in the number of people who had sex with multiple partners and an increase in celibacy among bisexual men. The researchers concluded that, at least in San

Francisco, bisexual men who were single 'do not appear to be a common vector for spreading HIV disease to women' (p.919).

This was also seen in *Dual Attraction: Understanding Bisexuality* (Pryor *et al.* 1994), where the people were also based in San Francisco, and numerous people talked about practising 'safe sex'. Some chose to use condoms for most or all of their sexual encounters. Others decided that monogamy and cutting out casual sex was the only way to remove the risk, while others used protection even in these relationships. Being selective with your partners and vetting them was also mentioned.

However, this may not necessarily be the case globally. In Chapter 11 of *Women in Relationships with Bisexual Men: Bi Men By Women*, Pallotta-Chiarolli (2016) discusses the sexual health issues that bisexual men face. She mentions that, internationally, a large proportion of bisexual men 'did not necessarily practice safe sex' and 'engaged in high risk sexual behaviours' (p.297).

But there are studies that show that bisexuality is not the super spreader of disease that the media would have you believe it is (Binson *et al.* 1997). As mentioned previously in Chapter 1, we must remember that HIV transmission can occur between heterosexual men and women. And there are other ways HIV can be transmitted, such as drug use.

It is important to not scapegoat m-spec men as the problem, label them as a vector of disease and claim they are bridging the gap between communities. Instead, we must understand the root cause of the issue and address it.

The impact of not coming out

What impact do stories like Todd's and those in *Dual Attraction* have on the sexual health of m-spec men? As we have already noted, even in the present day a large proportion of m-spec men simply do not come out. Whether with friends and family or healthcare professionals, m-spec men often hide their identity. Without disclosing their identity, are m-spec men getting access to the care that they need? Are the resources and information around safer sex reaching them?

Pallotta-Chiarolli (2016) states that the resistance from men to identify as gay or bisexual and the denial of their same-sex encounters may explain why bisexual men are not having safer sex. Those men who are not engaged with the gay community may not have access to the information around safe sex with men and 'therefore may have been putting themselves and their sexual partners at risk unwittingly' (p.297).

The resistance to identifying as m-spec among men who have sex with people of different genders is multi-layered. Some simply may not identify with this label. These men may have a heavy preference for women, both sexually and romantically, and desire a future with women. Meanwhile, they may also have sexual encounters with men which are often casual, fleeting and infrequent. These men may see themselves as straight and identify as such; therefore, the messaging around safer sex for m-spec men, men who have sex with men, and men who have sex with both men and women may not reach them.

I should make clear here that identity is what an individual makes of it. If these men see themselves as straight and identify as such, this is perfectly valid even if their sexual behaviour may point to other identities. However, it is also important to look at the barriers for these men to identify as something other than straight.

These men will have been brought up in a monosexist and heteronormative society. As a result, they may believe that m-spec identities do not exist and understand that if they were to disclose their attraction to men, they would be seen as gay. They know that this would lead to discrimination and the various hardships that come with that. We have seen how these structures play out in Chapter 2, and how they have prevented m-spec men from coming out.

There are various aspects of a person's life that are impacted when coming out, as we have discussed in the book thus far. One area that may be of particular interest here is dating and relationships. As we discussed in the dating and relationships chapter, m-spec men often struggle to gain the attention of women due to m-spec phobia. These men may be acutely aware of how they would be perceived if they were to come out as m-spec or even express their attraction or disclose their relations with regard to men. They may understand that they would be seen as gay and this would lock them out of relationships with women. While not all of these men may necessarily be more attracted to women, this may be the case for some and the reason for retaining a straight identity.

This idea is often used to demonize these men, blaming them for the spread of HIV. This is especially true of Black men, as mentioned previously in Chapter 1 on representation and education, as the media portrays them as 'down low'. While there is evidence to the contrary that m-spec men aren't the super spreaders of HIV, this is entirely beside the point. Demonizing m-spec men in this way is not helpful. All this does is create a stigma that stops m-spec men from being open, both about their HIV status and their identity. This causes increased barriers for m-spec men to get access to the help and resources they need. Instead, we should be understanding the issues that m-spec men face and finding ways to solve them.

Lack of research

Another major issue here is the lack of research. The long-standing problem of poor research into the issues that m-spec men face when it comes to HIV perpetuates a cycle where m-spec men are not getting the help, information, resources and care that they so clearly need.

As I discuss more in the chapter on Pride, many of our spaces, groups, communities and activism often fell under the banner of gay or lesbian and gay. This was also the case when it came to activism around HIV and AIDS. While m-spec people were part of this fight, something that Shearing (2021) discusses in her book, they did so under the banner of gay. As a result, m-spec people are often erased from the narrative.

Research around HIV and AIDS often focused on gay men. As Dodge and Feinstein (2020) state in their paper entitled 'Meeting the sexual health needs of bisexual men in the age of biomedical HIV prevention: Gaps and priorities', 'Historically, the field of HIV/STI prevention has primarily focused on addressing the sexual health needs of gay men (or "men who have sex with men [MSM]" as a broad category) with limited attention to the unique needs of bisexual men' (p.217).

Research on m-spec men often didn't ask the right questions, which meant it didn't help tackle the issues m-spec men were experiencing. Crawford, Kippax and Prestage (2020) looked at two large studies conducted in Australia: Project Male-Call and the BANGAR (Bisexual and Non-Gay Attached Research) Project. These studies examined the sexual acts of these behaviourally bisexual men, the level of intimacy they showed when having sex with men, where they had sex with men, their preferences, recent sexual history and so on. They also examined condom use in certain situations.

Yet it appears the researchers did not ask anything regarding why these behaviourally bisexual men were not connected to the gay community, the barriers they faced in doing so, the discrimination that they faced, the reason for hiding their sexual acts with men, and so on. They did not ask the right questions, and therefore did not fully capture the lived experiences of m-spec men and the way in which m-spec phobia and erasure impacted their lives. This naturally meant that no meaningful actions were created. Due to the failings of this research, there was no ammunition to fight for policy changes and get the funding necessary to fix the barriers for m-spec men. This is an issue that persists to this day.

M-spec phobia and erasure in LGBTQIA+ spaces

Dodge and Feinstein (2020) discuss various issues that bisexual men face when it comes to their sexual health. On the topic of pre-exposure prophylaxis (PrEP), a pill you can take to protect yourself from contracting HIV, they say:

> Research on PrEP has also not been intentionally inclusive of bisexual men, nor has it focused on their potentially unique PrEP-related concerns and needs. Many PrEP trials and studies have recruited and engaged participants from gay-oriented venues in large urban areas with well-established 'gay community' resources, which bisexual men are less likely to access due to anticipated and prior negative experiences related to stigma toward bisexuality from gay men. (p.224)

The m-spec phobia and erasure that m-spec people face within the LGBTQIA+ community is something I will look at further in the Pride chapter, but this highlights another layer of the issue we have seen thus far. For some men, the fact that they hide their sexual relations with men and don't come out as gay or m-spec creates a barrier for them. It means they are unlikely to enter LGBTQIA+ spaces where they can gain access to the resources they need to have safer sex.

But coming out doesn't necessarily solve the issue. Some m-spec men experience discrimination within LGBTQIA+ spaces, so much so that they avoid them. Therefore, they do not have access to the resources and the issue continues. And since research studies recruit from these spaces, they aren't finding m-spec men to include in the data. This means that the issues of m-spec men are not captured, so nothing is done to fix them.

This is called the cycle of invisibility (LGBTIQ+ Health Australia 2018). The discrimination and exclusion lead to no data on m-spec people, which means there is no awareness of their issues, so the questions on what can be done to help them go unasked. This leads to no perceived need to change, therefore zero policies on helping m-spec people and zero funding for these services. So exclusion is embedded in these systems, which leads to further exclusion and discrimination and the cycle just repeats itself.

This is systemic and structural monosexism in a nutshell, it is a self-perpetuating cycle that causes m-spec phobia and erasure that directly harm the lives of m-spec people. This doesn't just happen in regard to sexual health but in numerous parts of m-spec people's lives, as we have already discussed. But this is a clear, prime example of how the structure is created and upheld.

Related to this is the idea of 'exclusion by inclusion'. Pallotta-Chiarolli (2016) writes:

> This is evident in the way health organizations focusing on same-sex attraction gain funding for projects that appear to

be inclusive of bisexual people by including bisexuality as a category in their project outline and submissions. However, they do not follow through with bisexual-specific recommendations, outcomes or services. (pp.438–439)

While this was written in relation to mental health (and something we will discuss further in the Pride chapter), it also rings true here.

I have seen numerous health promotions, advertising campaigns, resources, services and more that mention 'bisexual'. It is common to see 'gay and bisexual men' in media related to HIV and STIs. But how much of this is actually reaching bisexual and m-spec people? Lumping these two groups together isn't always helpful – we have seen as much in this chapter (let alone the book as a whole). If, for example, these health promotions are only ever shown in LGBTQIA+ spaces, are m-spec people benefitting from them to the same degree?

Using 'gay and bisexual men' throughout an HIV awareness campaign is all well and good, but if the differences between the experiences of these groups are not understood and different approaches not created to target these demographics, then it's nothing more than a strapline. This is exclusion by inclusion: appearing to include bisexual and m-spec men on face value but doing nothing different to reach them, to actually help them.

Barriers to research

In *Recognize* (2015), Brian Dodge talks about the issues he experienced when trying to conduct research into bisexual men for his chapter 'Scientific Research on Bisexual Men: What Do We Know, and Why Don't We Know More?' Dodge talks about his time as a participant in a postdoctoral HIV-research training and how he 'encountered a very unexpected and unsettling resistance to understanding and accepting bisexuality as a valid sexual orientation, particularly among men' (p.119).

He was proposing a small 'pilot research study that was intended to explore issues related to HIV risk and sexual identity among bisexual men' (p.119). Dodge says that in the early 2000s, when he was trying to conduct this study, there was greater understanding of the significance of identity, discrimination and community. There was also knowledge that identity and behaviour didn't necessarily align and that individuals' sexual behaviours and partners varied throughout their life. Therefore, it seemed only logical to explore the lived experiences of bisexual men and how this interplayed with their risk of contracting HIV.

But Dodge found himself constantly rewriting, revising and reviewing his proposal due to the barriers he faced. He states that while some people in the HIV research world would say that men who have sex with men and women are the reason for HIV spreading from homosexual to heterosexual communities, they would swiftly follow this statement up with another stating that bisexual men do not exist.

And this became a blockade for Dodge. One grant reviewer, on reading Dodge's proposal, demanded evidence that bisexual men exist. Dodge revised the proposal, adding such evidence as well as a letter of support from Dr Fritz Klein, who detailed his own evidence in the matter of the existence of bisexual men. The grant reviewer did not find this evidence sufficient to back up the claim that bisexual men existed.

This essay from Dodge highlights yet another barrier. If those in positions of power to give grants and funding into research aren't willing to accept the existence of bisexual and m-spec men, then they aren't going to provide funding to allow research into the hardships of these men. This adds to the issue of the lack of research, which makes the cycle of invisibility harder to break.

Behaviour vs identity

In order to surmount this barrier, Dodge (2015) instead used the term 'men who have sex with both men and women (MSMW)' (p.122). He realized, with the help of his mentor Dr Theo Sandfort, that certain buzzwords needed to be avoided in order to gain and retain federal funding, and unfortunately bisexual was one of those words. Dodge worked within the system and was able to obtain the support necessary to undertake his important research.

Once Dodge had got his foot in the door, he was able to do the work he wanted to do from the outset and 'use the results as a form of resistance against the structures and systems that had pushed me down so far' (p.123). And Dodge has been part of numerous studies in this area, providing valuable insight into the lives of m-spec men.

In their paper 'Meeting the sexual health needs of bisexual men in the age of biomedical HIV prevention: Gaps and priorities', Dodge and Feinstein (2020) discuss the use of MSMW and the topic of sexual identity versus sexual behaviour. They say that while 'MSMW represents an important step toward understanding the sexual health needs of bisexual men, the category MSMW is not inclusive of all bisexual men' (p.217).

There are a number of issues with using solely a behavioural approach without taking identity into account, which Dodge and Feinstein outline. First, there are bisexual men who do not have sex with men and women and therefore their experiences are not included when looking at MSMW. Second, categories like MSMW are time dependent. Depending on the timeframe that is being observed, the category that a person belongs to can change. Third, it undermines self-determination. Ignoring the way in which the subject identifies means ignoring the issues they may face.

Another issue here is cissexism. Not only is the language very binary (men who have sex with men or men who have sex with men and women) and not inclusive of non-binary people but it also begs the question of who is included in these categories of men and women. The language often used in these HIV studies and the complete lack of acknowledgement of the specific challenges that trans men experience, which are likely to be different from cis men, point to potential exclusion of trans men from this research. In fact, Dodge and Feinstein state that 'transgender men are largely absent from the literature on HIV/STI prevention' (p.226).

It is important that identity here is considered because, as Dodge and Feinstein outline, the experience of those who may be behaviourally bisexual is going to be different from those who self-identify as bisexual. The latter may experience discrimination due to their identity that leads to increased hardship and creates barriers for resources and care that those who do not identify as bisexual may not experience.

On the flip side, the fact that bisexual men are more open about their identity means that they are more likely to be open about their sex lives and sexual experiences than those who are behaviourally bisexual but identify otherwise. This means they may have better access to communities, and therefore information and resources, than behaviourally bisexual (but not self-identified as bisexual) people.

So we can see that it is important to examine the issues faced by MSMW. It can give us insight into the struggles that they have, such as the inability to come out or disclose their sexual behaviour, and the way this can impact their access to information, resources and adequate care. But we must remember that the MSMW category is not congruent with m-spec. Identity and behaviour are separate and may or may not overlap for an individual. We must also accept that MSMW is an imperfect category that can be exclusionary. Taking a multi-layered approach to research can be a lot more revealing and can help with formulating better, more targeted health promotions for different demographics.

Women with m-spec men

In Dodge's chapter in *Recognize* (2015), he mentions something that is particularly noteworthy. After changing his language from bisexual to MSMW, he talks about a peer review meeting in which he was told, 'And think of the risks they pose to their female partners' (p.122). This highlights a recurring theme when discussing the issue of HIV and AIDS among bisexual and m-spec men; the focus is always on the women who may be in relationships with these men.

The health and wellbeing of m-spec men is consistently seen as unimportant and insignificant, something not worth exploring. Its importance is only found through the way that it may impact assumedly straight women in particular. We have seen this in the way article after article was produced around m-spec men being the bridge between communities. We can see here how the research was funded in part because of how their female partners are impacted. This can even explain why Pallotta-Chiarolli took the approach she did with her book (2016).

In the 1990s, there were several HIV promotions focused

around bisexual and m-spec men. These promotions all had a similar theme: they showed a man and a woman clearly in a relationship but showed the man was also having a relationship with another man, presumably without his female partner knowing. They also all had a bench. This became known as 'the bisexual bench' (Bi Stuff 2020). While there were similarities in the imagery, the text differed.

In the version from Oslo, the health promotion was clearly aimed at bisexual men. The translation from Bi Stuff shows that the advert aimed to inform bisexual men of their heightened risk of contracting HIV and to stress the importance of testing, as well as advertising services that they can access.

The Australian version, however, takes a very different approach. The text on this poster states 'Do you think your partner could be having sex with men? YOU ARE NOT ALONE' and then goes on to advertise 'The Women Partners of Bisexual Men Project' (Bi Stuff 2020). Instead of talking to bisexual and m-spec men, providing resources and services, they're instead targeting their women partners and painting these men as devious, deceitful cheaters. They had an entire community dedicated to women who were in a relationship with a bisexual man, but did they have anything for the men themselves? I think the answer is likely no.

It highlights how m-spec phobia and erasure are structural. In a society that is heteronormative, those who sit outside heterosexuality go uncared for. It is partly why the AIDS epidemic was allowed to tear through the LGBTQIA+ community in the way it did. And in a society that is monosexist, m-spec people are removed from the narrative and the few structures that are built to help non-heterosexual people are often not inclusive of m-spec people.

These systems clearly do not care about the health and

wellbeing of m-spec men because they do not care about m-spec men full stop. It is only when we supposedly pose a threat to heterosexual people that suddenly we become noticed and, even then, the focus is on the threat we pose rather than the hardship we are experiencing.

Impact on m-spec men's sexual health

What we have discussed thus far now has given us a clear picture of the structures that m-spec men are up against. M-spec men struggle to come out and those who do face bigotry even within the LGBTQIA+ community, which means they are not present in LGBTQIA+ spaces. This means that they do not have access to the information they need, meaning they lack the knowledge of the risks involved and how to navigate and engage in sex with people of multiple genders in a safer manner. The lack of research and barriers to conducting said research around m-spec men means these issues aren't understood and so no action is taken to fill this gap, and m-spec men remain uninformed.

What is the impact of this? Dodge and Feinstein (2020) high-light numerous ways in which the sexual health of bisexual men is impacted. They reference numerous studies that show that 'bisexual men may be less likely to receive HIV/STI prevention information than gay men', 'that bisexual men are less likely to get tested for HIV/STI than gay men and that they get tested less frequently' and that 'bisexual men are less likely to use PrEP than gay men' (p.220).

They also note studies that focused more on MSMW rather than self-identified bisexual men, but these studies showcased numerous issues too. They showed that 'HIV-positive MSMW are less likely to be aware of their HIV-positive status and to receive HIV care', 'less likely to be virally suppressed', 'more likely to experience later HIV diagnoses' and 'more likely to receive an AIDS diagnosis within 1–3 years of initial HIV diagnosis' when compared to HIV-positive men who have sex with men only (MSMO) (p.224). They also note a study that looked at both self-identified bisexual men and behaviourally bisexual men and found much the same outcomes.

This shows the very real impact of m-spec phobia and erasure and the profound effect it has on the sexual health of m-spec men. This link has even been highlighted by the CDC (Cruz 2014).

Sexual health clinics

While we have spoken about the barriers that m-spec men face in regards to coming out and accessing LGBTQIA+ spaces, and the way this prevents them from accessing information and resources, those m-spec men who are informed about safer sex options face further barriers still. As we discussed in the introduction to this health chapter, m-spec men experience issues from health professionals when accessing care. From not understanding their specific needs to inappropriate questions, the care that m-spec men receive leaves much to be desired.

Kamal told me that when he was sexually active with people of multiple genders, he had to advocate really hard to get medical professionals to understand his sexuality and test him appropriately. He recalled a time when he brought up the HPV vaccine to a nurse at a sexual health clinic and was met with confusion. The nurse was only aware of Kamal sleeping with men. On explaining that Kamal slept with people of multiple genders, the confusion turned to disgust.

Alan is a bi non-binary person and their partner is a bi cis woman. They told me that when visiting sexual health clinics, they often put down 'male' for simplicity. They told me of an experience they had once when visiting the clinic with their partner where their partner disclosed to the nurse that Alan was bisexual. On doing so, Alan's partner was told she was at a heightened risk because 'your partner sleeps with men'.

Men who sleep with men are treated as a high-risk group by NHS sexual health services and since Alan had stated that they were a man, Alan and, by extension, their partner, was seen as high risk. When Alan's partner clarified the situation and said that Alan was not having sex with men, the nurse asked, 'How does that work?' Alan and their partner understood this question to mean, 'How can someone be bi and not have sex with people of multiple genders?'

After this appointment, Alan told me that their partner received a phone call on two occasions stating that she was at a high risk due to Alan's sexuality. They told her that she should get the hepatitis vaccine, a vaccine ordinarily only offered to men who have sex with men.

Alan also told me of a time when they ordered an STI home-testing kit for themselves and their partner. Alan's test included both a throat and an anal swab, despite never having engaged in anal sex, while their partner's test had neither.

What these experiences highlight is a lack of understanding by these healthcare professionals about what it means to be m-spec. It means they make assumptions based on the person's sexuality, which could be incorrect. This results in poor care service for these individuals that ends up stigmatizing them. This can result in many of these individuals not returning, which leads to lack of testing among m-spec men and worsened health outcomes.

Instead of these assumptions, these healthcare professionals should be having open conversations with these individuals about the sexual behaviours they are engaging in. This means they can undertake the relevant tests and provide the required information. They can then use this as a jumping-off point to provide other information that may also be relevant due to their identity and attraction, ensuring the individual is well informed should their behaviour change in the future.

People living with HIV

What impact does this structure have on those who are living with HIV? I spoke to Steve, who was diagnosed with HIV in late 2018, after coming out as bisexual earlier in the year and having identified as gay for most of his life (from the age of 13). Due to this diagnosis, Steve put his embracing of his bisexuality on hold to focus on his diagnosis.

Steve encountered numerous issues in navigating his HIV diagnosis as a bisexual man. When Steve was diagnosed, his doctor filled out a form regarding his behaviour during the period of exposure. For Steve, this was three months and during this time he had only had sex with a couple of men. This meant that Steve was coded as homosexual in that data rather than bisexual. He was never asked his identity and so he found himself completely erased. This highlights why data around HIV rates often lumps gay and bisexual men together. In fact, it is solely based around behaviour which is, incorrectly, translated to gay and bisexual.

Steve said that he often finds his bisexuality completely erased in HIV spaces and finds himself fighting not just for himself but all m-spec men. Steve works in the HIV sector and finds that across community, policy and research, m-spec men are lumped in with gay men as men who have sex with men (MSM). He finds that programmes for people living with HIV often cater either for straight men or gay men, with nothing specifically for m-spec men. He said that even when groups say that they're for gay and bisexual men, they are actually only really for gay men.

When Steve was first diagnosed with HIV, he attended a gay male group programme for recently diagnosed people. When he spoke up and said that he was actually bi rather than gay, he was met with mocking laughs from about half the room. When he asked questions around anatomy that wasn't related to cis gay men, he found himself either dismissed or met with, 'I'll look into that for you'.

This highlights how these spaces clearly aren't well equipped to deal with the issues that m-spec men living with HIV face. Yet again, we see that m-spec men are not meaningfully included within these spaces, so they are unable to get the education that they need and therefore do not attend these spaces due to the discrimination, poor understanding and lack of inclusion they experience.

Steve has experienced a high level of stigma, discrimination and abuse since being diagnosed with HIV. He has had nurses double-gloving when having to examine and test him to getting death threats on apps like Grindr. Having to deal with this on top of m-spec phobia and erasure creates yet another barrier to accessing resources and can be severely damaging to someone's mental wellbeing.

I spoke to Khafre, a Black bisexual man who was diagnosed with HIV in 1989. He had been having unprotected sex with both men and women at the time and thought it best to get tested, especially as he was hoping to ask the woman he was dating to marry him. His diagnosis rocked him to his core and he saw the future he had planned for himself disappear. He felt incredibly isolated and scared, so much so that he didn't share his diagnosis with anyone, apart from the woman he was dating, for six years.

Khafre has written further about his experiences during this time. In an article for H-I-V.net, Khafre said that after being diagnosed, he thought the woman he loved wouldn't want to marry him and he would never have kids (Abif 2019). The shame and stigma clearly impacted his outlook on life, which deeply affected his mental health.

Khafre eventually did open up about his diagnosis and sought treatment. He also started to attend a support group specifically for gay and bisexual men who were living with HIV. This support group helped him out of a dark place, allowing him to shed the fear and shame around his diagnosis, which gave him the strength he needed to tell his loved ones about his diagnosis. This shows the power that support groups can have, and the importance of making these groups fully inclusive of bi and m-spec men. It can help save lives, as it did with Khafre.

There are some parallels between the stigma that people living with HIV experience and m-spec phobia and erasure. Both of these, Steve told me, have an aspect of mistrust. M-spec people are often seen as untrustworthy, as lying about their sexuality. Similarly, those living with HIV are seen to be lying about the fact that they're undetectable and can't pass HIV on. Those who are both m-spec and living with HIV are constantly treated as suspicious.

HIV stigma goes beyond this though. Steve told me that he believes a lot of the stigma around HIV stems from the epidemic and intergenerational trauma, which is different from the source of m-spec phobia. He believes this is what fuels a lot of the hatred that people living with HIV face.

Information

As we can see throughout this section, the systematic discrimination of m-spec identities has created numerous barriers for m-spec men to get help, information and resources to manage their sexual health. With that in mind, I will end this section with some vital information around HIV, testing and safer sex in the hope that it will assist you in navigating your sexual health.

I should state that I am not a sexual health professional or medical professional in any regard. This is information I have mostly learned through navigating and looking after my own sexual health, as well as engaging, helping and assisting with grassroots organizational efforts around awareness and research for my own health as well as for this book. I have mentioned and linked numerous resources below that can hopefully provide more information. I hope that this provides the groundwork to allow you to look after your sexual health.

PrEP stands for pre-exposure prophylaxis and it is a pill you can take to protect yourself from HIV. The efficacy of PrEP is about 99 per cent (CDC, n.d.). There are a number of different ways that you can take PrEP:

- Daily – take one pill a day.
- On demand/event based – take two pills 2–24 hours before sex, one pill 24 hours after sex and one more pill 24 hours after that. If you are having sex over a period of time, keep taking a pill every 24 hours until you have two sex-free days.
- Ts and Ss – four pills a week every Tuesday, Thursday, Saturday and Sunday. It is recommended to first take a daily pill for seven days and then drop down to four a week.

- Holiday PrEP – take one pill daily for seven days before you go away, one pill a day for each day during the period you are away and then one pill daily for seven days following said period.

It is important to note that if you are having vaginal or frontal sex, you must take one pill a day. On demand and Ts and Ss do not provide adequate protection if you are having vaginal or frontal sex, only for anal sex. Both Holiday, which is essentially Daily but for a certain period of time, and Daily both provide adequate protection for vaginal or frontal sex.

The lead-in time for PrEP is seven days. So, if you are taking PrEP Daily, it will take seven days to become effective. This is also why for Holiday and Ts and Ss it is recommended to take one pill a day for seven days to start. It is important to note that PrEP is only used to protect you from HIV. It cannot protect you from chlamydia, gonorrhea, syphilis or any other sexually transmitted diseases/infections (STDs/STIs).

PrEP can be obtained on the NHS in the UK, thanks to the many grassroots organizations who fought for its provision. In the US, there are many different ways to source PrEP, and if you have insurance, you may be able to get a prescription for it. If not, there are programmes like Ready, Set, PrEP (HIV.gov) which you may be eligible for. Visit your healthcare provider, community health centre, sexual health clinic or governmental health clinic to find more. There are also ways to purchase PrEP online without a prescription, although you may need to check whether this is legal or not in your area. Check out www.iwantprepnow. co.uk for more information on how to buy and use PrEP.

PrEP, at least in the UK, should be available for anyone who wants and needs it. The focus is often on gay and bisexual cis men, but trans men and women, regardless of sexuality, are also eligible and PrEP is safe to take with hormones. Availability is often for those who are having, or planning to have, unprotected sex so take note of this if you wish to access PrEP. Those having sex with someone who is HIV+ who is not on treatment are also eligible for PrEP. For others, it is still worth talking to someone at a clinic about accessing PrEP, especially if you believe that you could be at risk.

You also need to be HIV negative in order to access PrEP. They will often run a full test screening to check for hepatitis B and any STDs/STIs, and to ensure that you are HIV negative. They will also check your kidney function to ensure you can take PrEP. For more information on PrEP, how to take it, eligibility, procedures and more visit your local health clinic, www.iwantprepnow.co.uk or https://prepster.info. This is where I learned most, if not all, of the information I have relayed above.

For other STDs/STIs, condoms are very effective (around 98%) and protect against most STDs/STIs such as chlamydia and gonorrhea (Get The Facts, n.d.). However, they cannot protect against all STDs/STIs. Those that are transmitted via skin to skin contact such as herpes, syphilis, HPV, molluscum and crabs can still be transmitted (Winderl 2016). STDs/STIs can also be transmitted through oral sex and you can use condoms or a dental dam for this (Holland 2019). Speaking from personal experience, however, protection often isn't used during oral sex. Condoms are not just for people with a penis as there are also 'female condoms' which can be used by those with a vagina. These are seen to be 95 per cent effective and can also protect against STDs/STIs (NHS, n.d.).

For some STDs/STIs, you can get vaccines to help protect you from contracting them. There are vaccines available for HPV, hepatitis A and hepatitis B for those men who have sex with men (Prepster, n.d.). Talk to your local sexual health clinic for more information and to get these vaccines.

Getting regularly tested is incredibly important. Unfortunately, I cannot help much in regard to the discrimination that you may face when you interact with sexual health services. Home-testing kits, if they are available in your area, can at least limit interaction but assumptions can still be made about your behaviours, as seen in Alan's case. Testing regularly can help you catch any STDs/STIs early, which can help you get treatment before your condition worsens. For those on PrEP, you are often given three months of dosage and are asked to return to the clinic every three months to get tested and receive more PrEP.

How often you get tested entirely depends on how often you get sex. If you are having sex often and/or with multiple partners, it is often recommended to get tested every one to three months. If you are having sex less often, every three to six months is more reasonable. If you've just had a new encounter, getting tested afterwards is often a good idea. It is worth noting that some STDs/STIs take time to show up on tests, so getting tested immediately after having sex will not always give an accurate result. You also may not always present with symptoms, so getting tested is important even if there is nothing wrong. If you are in a committed monogamous relationship, you may not need to get tested as frequently, but it is always worth visiting the clinic on occasion to ensure your health is okay. For more information on testing, talk to someone at your nearest sexual health clinic or read more at online sites, such as Your Sexual Health (2020).

If you have just had unprotected sex, are not on PrEP and are concerned about HIV, there is an option available. PEP, which stands for post-exposure prophylaxis, is a month-long course of HIV drugs that you can take if you are concerned about being exposed to HIV (www.iwantprepnow.co.uk). This treatment needs to start within 72 hours, ideally within 24 hours. You can access PEP from your local sexual health clinic or from A&E in the UK. In the US, you can access PEP from the emergency room, local sexual health clinic, Planned Parenthood and some doctors' offices (Planned Parenthood, n.d.).

If you do test positive for HIV, there is antiretroviral medicine available that you can take in order to fight the virus. While HIV is currently not curable, it is not the death sentence it used to be. As long as you are on effective treatment, you are able to live a long life. Better than this, if you are on effective treatment, you can reduce the viral load to such low levels that it becomes undetectable. And if you are undetectable, then you are unable to transmit the virus to others. So undetectable = untransmittable (U=U) (Kasadha 2019). This is called treatment as prevention (TasP), which means taking treatment for HIV in order to prevent passing it on (Avert, n.d.).

It is incredibly important that this is understood. People living with HIV often experience undue hardship because of the stigma surrounding the disease. This can lead to worsened health outcomes for those living with HIV, such as mental health issues. Education is only part of the battle here, however. Steve told me that he often received messages of hate and had been stigmatized by those who are on PrEP, people who would have received education on how PrEP protects them and on antiretroviral medication.

This hatred is completely irrational. We must change the way we view those who are living with HIV and unlearn the idea that contracting HIV leads to death. There are many who live long, fulfilling lives who are HIV+ and on treatment. We must ensure that we do not perpetuate this stigma and must work to create an environment where people can talk about their status openly and gain access to the help and resources necessary to look after their health.

We must also acknowledge the fact that if it wasn't for those living with HIV, both historically and presently, putting in the hard work to push governments to address HIV, we wouldn't be where we are today. It is thanks to their tireless work that we have access to medication, both antiretroviral medicine and PrEP, that our community has the resources, networks and support we do have and that we're informed on things like U=U. And, thanks to those living with HIV who got tested and are on effective treatment, we have managed to reduce HIV transmission.

But all of that is not the reason we should be fighting HIV stigma. We need to acknowledge that no medication is 100 per cent effective and transmission can happen, but also someone being irresponsible isn't a reason to stigmatize them. It is important to acknowledge the efforts made by those living with HIV while also ensuring that respect is not conditional on the basis of what they do. We must fight HIV stigma because of the impact it poses: it causes people to avoid getting tested, to hide their status, to refuse medication, to damage their mental health and even leads to death, which is all so preventable.

The Health of M-spec Men

I hope that this chapter has helped inform you about the impact that m-spec phobia and erasure have on the health and wellbeing of m-spec men – how they create barriers to research, limit access to resources and information, and reduce quality of care. The issues that m-spec men face go beyond interpersonal relations, beyond discrimination from friends and family, colleagues and lovers. This is a structural issue that can lead to unnecessary loss of life.

It is so important that we work to create a space that can

provide m-spec men with the care they so desperately need. I hope that some of the information and resources I have provided here can help lay some groundwork to working towards the betterment of m-spec men's health, but so much more needs to be done if we are to reduce the harm that is currently being caused.

CHAPTER 5

Intersectionality

As we have seen throughout the book thus far, m-spec phobia and erasure are pervasive in society and cause a detriment to the lives of numerous m-spec men. The lack of representation and education has helped enforce a binary construction of sexuality, making things like coming out or dating incredibly difficult for m-spec men. These issues impact m-spec men's mental health and can be hard to overcome when they face discrimination from even the support networks.

These issues can worsen for those who hold multiple identities at once. The term intersectionality is often used to help describe this issue. The term was coined by Kimberlé Crenshaw, an activist and legal scholar, to describe the specific oppression experienced by Black women (Perlman 2018). She discussed how 'traditional feminist ideas and antiracist policies exclude black women because they face overlapping discrimination unique to them' (Perlman 2018).

The use of this term has since been broadened. In Kimberlé Crenshaw's own words, intersectionality is 'a metaphor for understanding the ways multiple forms of inequality or disadvantage sometimes compound themselves and they create obstacles that often are not understood within conventional ways of thinking' (National Association of Independent Schools 2018).

There are numerous ways that this can play out in the lives of m-spec men, for instance when race issues intersect with m-spec identities. M-spec men of colour are subjected not only to m-spec phobia and erasure, but also to racism. They have to navigate both of these struggles simultaneously.

For example, according to Stonewall, 62 per cent of Black, Asian and minority ethnic (BAME) LGBT people stated that they experienced depression (2018), and 59 per cent of bi people reported experiencing depression (2020). For someone who is both bi and a person of colour, this could compound and they may be more likely to experience depression than those belonging to just one group.

Another intersection to consider is gender identity with m-spec identities. Transphobia is rampant in society, with some high-profile celebrities frequently using their platform to spread hate towards trans people. Naturally, the experiences that trans m-spec men have to deal with are going to differ drastically from cis m-spec men.

Again, if we look at statistics from Stonewall (2018), we can see that 61 per cent of LGBT people said they had experienced anxiety. When we drill further into this statistic, we can see that 71 per cent of trans people and 56 per cent of bi men said they experienced anxiety. You can see how this could compound and worsen for those belonging to both groups.

Often people see sexual and romantic attraction as one and the same, but this isn't the case. Attraction is complex and can present itself in many different forms. Some m-spec men may be asexual or on the asexual spectrum (ace-spec), meaning they may experience little to no sexual attraction but also experience multi-gendered romantic attraction. The reverse can also be true. Some m-spec men can be aromantic or on the aromantic spectrum (aro-spec), meaning they experience little to no romantic attraction but also experience multi-gendered sexual attraction. Asexuality and aromantic are often forgotten parts of the LGBTQIA+ community. Often people use 'LGBTQ+', burying them under the plus sign. Even when using LGBTQIA+, some incorrectly think of the A as ally.

A lot of research into the LGBTQIA+ community often doesn't discuss ace-spec or aro-spec – collectively referred to as a-spec – people. The many reports from Stonewall that I have mentioned throughout this book cover a variety of areas and provide numerous statistics on the struggles of LGBTQIA+ people in the UK. But in all the reports, I have not seen a single mention of a-spec people. It appears they were not surveyed for these reports at all.

However, there are some statistics out there. Unicorn March produced a report that collated various statistics that included asexual and ace-spec people (Unicorn March, n.d.). This report shows that people on the asexual spectrum experience high levels of discrimination and violence, high levels of mental health problems and high levels of homelessness. The statistics for this group are on par with, or sometimes greater than, those for m-spec people and this is often the group that is the worst off.

Not only do the problems that occur in both or all of the minority groups compound, making the people who belong to both worse off than those who only belong to one, but new obstacles can arise. For example, m-spec people may rely on LGBTQIA+ or m-spec safe spaces in order to fully embrace themselves, express who they are and gain support. However, is this a place that is safe for m-spec people of colour? Similarly, people of colour may form bonds with those from their cultural community but is this attainable for queer people? None of these spaces may be fully accessible to people who belong to multiple communities. Discrimination may rear its ugly head, blocking these people from the support that they would otherwise be able to get if they belonged to just a single community.

There are many more intersectional identities that we could cover and explore; however, I will be focusing on these three. We will discuss how living within these intersections creates new barriers and obstacles that can feel insurmountable to overcome and the impact this can have on people.

M-spec and Trans

Transphobia is extremely prevalent in today's society. According to the BBC, transphobic hate crimes in the UK have quadrupled in the last five years (Francis 2020) and increased by 81 per cent in 2017–2018 compared to the previous year (BBC 2019). Trans people face numerous barriers when it comes to equality, from access to healthcare to protection from discrimination. According to Stonewall, trans people experienced anxiety and suicidal ideation above the average levels for the LGBT community (2018a).

It is clear that trans people are an extremely vulnerable group. Their hyper-visibility within the media has caused an incredibly high and toxic backlash that has even seen high-profile figures, such as JK Rowling, jump on the bandwagon.

How do these issues worsen for trans men who are also m-spec? How do these identities play off one another and create new issues?

Gender essentialism

Gender essentialism is the idea that sex and gender are the same thing. It says that what makes someone a man or a woman is inherent, usually based on biological differences, normally chromosomal (Abrams 2020). This is what gives a person their 'essence' and determines their attributes and traits, such as their genitals, their strength, their emotional capability and so on (Jakubowski 2018).

This idea is often used by trans exclusionary radical feminists, essentially transphobes who use the veil of feminism to justify their actions. They believe that gender and sex are one and the same and are immutable; you cannot change your chromosomes and therefore you cannot change the gender that you were assigned at birth.

With this idea, they believe that trans people pose a risk to them. They believe that 'men who identify as women', the term they used to describe trans women, are going to invade women's spaces and therefore put them at risk of being harmed. That these 'men' are going to be allowed into women's toilets, women-only prisons and women-only refuges for domestic abuse survivors (Bull *et al.* 2021). This, they believe, puts women at risk of being abused or sexually assaulted by people they determine are men (Hilton and Wright 2020).

There is also a fear that trans people will cause cis women to transition. They are worried that women may be pressured or convinced that they can transition out of womanhood and thereby escape the harm that women face in society, namely sexism and misogyny (Burns 2019). This poses a risk to women, especially lesbians.

Get The L Out is a self-proclaimed lesbian feminist activist group which marched, uninvited, at the front of Pride In London in 2018 (Masson 2019). Their goal is to remove the L from the LGBTQIA+ community as they believe that trans activism is leading to lesbian erasure.

The belief is that lesbians may be convinced that they are actually men and need to transition as a result. Similar to the idea that women may transition to escape misogyny, there is a belief that lesbians will be convinced to transition and become straight trans men in order to escape structural homophobia (Burns 2019). There is also a concern that women 'who don't conform to sexist stereotypes', whether lesbian or not, will be told that they're men due to their lack of femininity and told to transition (Get The L Out UK, n.d.).

They believe that all of this results in lesbian erasure. They say that 'The LGBT community is coercing lesbians to accept penises as female organs and heterosexual intercourse as a lesbian sexual practice', denying lesbians' right to be same-sex attracted (Get The L Out UK, n.d.). They oppose this 'manipulative ideology' on the grounds that it is a 'form of rape culture aimed at lesbians, as well as a form of conversion therapy' (Get The L Out UK, n.d.).

They also say that forcing women who do not conform to traditional gender roles and sexist stereotypes to transition is a 'form of misogynist medical abuse against lesbians' and state the numerous ways it can harm women and girls (Get The L Out UK, n.d.). This is also often seen as a form of conversion therapy, as a lesbian is forced to become a straight man (Burns 2019). But no one is forcing lesbians or gender non-conforming women to do anything. It is completely ignoring 'the bodily autonomy of transmasculine people' (Burns 2019) and, as Hulme (2019) says, treating trans men as 'just foolish women whose words cannot have any value', simply brainwashed into thinking they are men (Burns 2019).

Cisnormativity

Cisnormativity is the assumption that all human beings are cisgender, that their gender matches that which they were assigned at birth. It is the structural privileging of cis people above others, namely trans people, and seeing cis as being the only valid identity. Cisnormativity is ingrained in our society and it is responsible for cissexism, which is the upholding of oppressive structural systems that impact trans people, and transphobia, which is the direct discrimination that trans people experience in everyday life (Clements 2021).

And it is this structure that gives us ideologies such as gender essentialism. Since there is a societal belief that being cis is the only way of existing, people believe that your gender must align with sex characteristics that were observable when you were born.

The argument often used is 'biology not bigotry', but in fact such arguments are anything but scientific (Burns 2019). Often transphobic people use very rudimentary science they picked up during their time at school: XY for a man and XX for a woman. Men have penises and produce sperm, while women have vaginas and produce eggs. Simple.

However, as outlined in articles by Sun (2019) and Ainsworth (2018) from *Scientific American*, both gender and sex exist on a spectrum. Biology is not as simple as these transphobic people will lead you to believe, since chromosomes, hormones, sex anatomy and brain structure can all vary. These simplistic notions of biology not only harm trans people, but also intersex people as they are often given medical procedures in order to force their bodies to comply with a specific sex.

Whether biology supports the existence of trans people or not is beside the point. As Greenesmith, one of Burns's (2019) interviewees says, 'Biology has been used as bigotry as long as biology has been a thing.' So stating 'biology not bigotry' is a flawed argument from the outset, as a belief could be both. Further to this, what biology actually says is of little to no importance to transphobic people. As outlined by Riley Black in her article for Slate (Black 2021), these people are 'not dealing in facts'.

We shouldn't be drawn into debates about what is or isn't scientifically true in order to justify the existence of trans people. It shouldn't matter. As Black mentions, 'trans rights are not a scientific issue. They are a human rights issue' (Black 2021). Trans people are people and deserve the same level of respect granted to cis people.

Conflation of identity

The result of these structures is a conflation between gender identity, gender expression and sexuality. As we have seen, transphobes often believe that trans people are working to convince lesbians and gender non-conforming women that they are trans men and to get them to transition.

But this is often missing the fact that trans people aren't necessarily straight, nor do they always conform to the rigid stereotypes of their gender (as transphobes often believe they do). A trans man can be feminine, he can be gay, straight, bisexual or anything else. A trans woman can be a lesbian, she can be masculine. Trans people are like everyone else, unique and varied individuals.

However, when transphobes do recognize the multiplicity of trans identities, they weaponise this to further the bigotry towards trans people. As mentioned earlier, there are those who claim that trans women are trying to convert lesbians into being straight by making them 'accept penises as female organs and heterosexual intercourse as a lesbian sexual practice' (Get The L Out UK, n.d.). This conspiratorial thinking boils down to a complete denial of trans people's identity, not just their gender but their sexuality as well.

From the m-spec men I spoke to, this conflation and denial of their identities was an incredibly common occurrence.

T told me that while he knew he was bisexual, he denied his feelings as his only understanding of m-spec identities was gay people using it to deny their true identity. He decided to settle on being a gay woman as he was more attracted to women and found himself drawn to the freedom that queer women appeared to have when expressing their gender identity.

Eventually, T came out as trans only to be confronted with this conflation between gender and sexuality. On learning of T's trans identity, his family incorrectly joined the dots and believed his attraction to women and his desire to dress 'like a man' was because he was a straight man the whole time. While T is into women, trans and dresses 'masculine', these are separate parts of his identity.

T said that this false impression his family had of his identity meant that they were finally able to accept him and make room for him in the family. This made T incredibly frightened that if he were to say anything about the true nature of his sexuality, he would be rejected. This impacted T's ability to accept and care for himself, which has damaged his mental health, and this has only worsened since T has returned back home. Since he relies on his family for support with his health issues, he is fearful that coming out to his family as bisexual could put this at risk.

Phillip said that after he came out as trans, he experienced quite a few people making this conflation. He recalled one person saying that now that he was a guy, they could go to the stadium and watch football together, prompting Phillip to explain that their interests had not changed and they still didn't like football.

Phillip found that a lot of people were either confused about his gender or assumed he now liked girls. At the time, Phillip was not interested in multiple genders and therefore was not out as m-spec. He informed said people that trans people, just like cis people, can be gay. While these comments show clear misunderstanding, Phillip said they were not ill-intentioned and found that most people, if not everyone, were incredibly supportive.

Jameson told me that when he came out as trans, he did fall out with a few friends. While they were transitioning, one friend insisted that they looked like a cute lesbian. When Jameson explained that this wasn't a compliment because he wasn't a woman, this friend told him he was being lesbophobic, that is, he was being negative or bigoted towards lesbians. This, of course, was not the case. Jameson is a non-binary trans man, not a lesbian. He isn't a woman. So being told that he is a gay woman is not a compliment and is misgendering him; it is transphobic.

This isn't an isolated case either. Jameson has experienced quite a bit of transphobia from the idea that it is lesbophobic to be a trans man. Some people believe that identifying as a trans man is just a roundabout way to say that it is shameful to be a lesbian. This specific brand of transphobia comes from within the LGBTQIA+ community, as we saw with Get The L Out earlier. Jameson said that this was made even more ridiculous by the fact that they never identified as a lesbian and if they still identified as a woman, they definitely would not be a lesbian.

Access to trans-related healthcare

This conflation from your peers, your family and your friends is just one part to this. It exists in every facet of society and can impact trans people's ability to access the care that they need when it comes to their physical and mental wellbeing, especially around trans-related healthcare.

Historically, sexual orientation was part of the criteria that had to be met for trans people to transition (Gardner 2019). This meant that for trans men to be recognized as men and receive the treatment they needed, they had to be attracted to women. This resulted in trans people being rejected from gender-affirming healthcare and surgery.

One of the people who was rejected on these grounds was Lou Sullivan. Lou was a trans activist in the US and one of the key players who helped remove this criterion to access trans healthcare. In an interview with Ira B. Pauly, Sullivan discussed how gender professionals would tell him how there was 'no such thing as a female to gay male' (Megan Rohrer 2010). He told Pauly how these professionals equated gender and sexuality when they are two separate issues and since heterosexual is seen as the norm, they believed that if they were 'going to make somebody better that means we have to make them heterosexual' (Megan Rohrer 2010).

While the criterion to be straight has been removed from the requirements to access gender-affirming healthcare, the expectation still exists. Numerous people I spoke to told me that they had either directly experienced discrimination and barriers to healthcare due to not being straight, or they had heard of others experiencing problems in this area. Many told me how they felt there was a pressure to conform to certain expectations of what it meant to be a man, whether this be their sexuality or their gender expression, in order to avoid any issues when accessing gender-affirming healthcare.

CJ told me that when he went for his initial hormone replacement therapy (HRT) appointment, he lied about being bisexual as he was worried about being discriminated against. He told me that he had heard of people being denied access to transition-related healthcare if they were not straight.

Will told me that the doctor at the gender identity clinic assumed that he was heterosexual because he spoke about an ex-girlfriend. Will corrected the doctor on this and the response he received was, 'Well, normal transsexuals are all straight'. After Will mentioned his current boyfriend, the doctor asked whether he was cis or trans. Will stated he was trans, prompting the doctor to ask whether he was on hormones. When Will confirmed that his boyfriend was not on hormones, the doctor responded with 'So you *are* straight'.

This shows how these bigoted views don't just exist among the general public but even among healthcare professionals, including the very professionals who are supposed to be helping trans people. Too often, these professionals create a new barrier for trans people that they have to overcome in order to access the help they need.

Phillip told me how during his transition, he needed to get two reports from psychologists confirming he was trans in order to get his name changed as well as access gender-affirming surgery. This was a huge battle for Phillip. They were asked numerous personal questions and they found that even therapists who specialized in trans people believed that a trans person needed to perfectly fit cisnormative gender ideals, which included being 100 per cent straight.

He noted that a number of therapists raised concerns over him being bisexual, clearly seeing it as a red flag. Phillip said that while they may have received similar reactions if he was gay, these therapists seemed especially perturbed by the fact that they were attracted to multiple genders.

Subverting binaries

The experience that Phillip had is incredibly significant. In her book Bi: *Notes for a Bisexual Revolution* (2013), Shiri Eisner explains the common ground between m-spec people and trans people, stating that 'the most obvious common ground that bisexuality and transgender share is that of subverting binaries' (p.240).

As we have already stated, we live in a world that is both monosexist and cissexist. Our society works in binaries and believes that the only valid sexualities are gay and straight. Likewise, our society believes that everyone is cisgender, that your gender and sex are one and the same and everyone is either a man or a woman. M-spec identities and trans identities upset the status quo. M-spec identities upset the gay/straight binary while trans identities upset the man/woman binary.

Both m-spec and trans also threaten the idea of essentialism, that you are 'born a certain way (male, female, gay, straight) and cannot change' by offering 'the options of mutability and change' (Eisner 2013, p.241). As Eisner explains, if you look at an m-spec or trans person at a single moment in their life, you may see them as one sexuality/gender, but by taking a long-term view, you may open up other possibilities.

As Shearing discusses in her book, the 'born this way' argument that is often used in the LGBTQIA+ community, while having done a lot of good for LGBTQIA+ rights, leaves a lot of 'queer people out in the cold' (2021, p.64). She says that it gives the impression that we would be straight and cis if we could and that our identities are fixed, set in stone, rather than giving room to the idea that sexuality and gender are fluid and can change and develop.

Living in a cissexist society means that there is often a lack of education about and awareness of trans identities. But as awareness of trans identities grows and we create an environment that allows and accepts trans people, we may find that more people discover that they are trans and may decide to transition. This isn't trans people 'forcing' or 'brainwashing' people, as the transphobes would argue, but people becoming aware of new options, new possibilities, that are available to them and exploring them. When we hold on to this idea that identity is innate, we remove the idea that change is possible, which it very much is. We must take into account the way in which our society, our environment and our experiences impact us.

Confusion of identity

Another part of this conflation could be due to the implicit inversion theory. If you recall from previous chapters, implicit inversion theory is the societal belief that the gender expression of a person is connected to their sexual orientation and vice versa. So men who appear feminine are seen to be gay, for example. This means that the idea of what it means to be masculine, what it means to be a man, is heavily tied up in heterosexuality.

With this in mind, it stands to reason that society would believe that someone who desires to transition to a man would also present as masculine and be straight. Society has wrapped up gender and sexuality into one package, so a trans man who is not straight is not understood. To be a man is to be attracted to women; if they aren't or are also attracted to other genders, then the question aimed at them is: Are you sure you're a man?

This creates the argument that they may be confused, which is another similarity with the experiences of m-spec people. When it comes to medical professionals there is a fear that they may misdiagnose someone as trans, resulting in irreparable and irreversible damage, and when these trans people eventually detransition, the blame for the damage caused will be placed squarely at their feet.

But as statistics in the UK from 2016–2017 show, 'Less than one per cent said in those appointments that they had experienced transitioned-related regret, or had detransitioned' (Medcalf 2019). This doesn't take into account factors such as people discovering their identity through transition or issues surrounding family, housing or work. Regret could also stem from various places, such as unsatisfactory surgery results.

Statistics from the US show similar results. While 8 per cent of respondents reported detransitioning, 62 per cent stated it was temporary (Knox 2019). It was seen that pressure from a parent was the most common reason for detransitioning, while only 0.4 per cent responded saying they realized transitioning was not right for them.

From this, it is clear that the vast majority of trans people who transition benefit from doing so. It is exceedingly rare to see people who detransition or experience regret from transitioning, and the reasons for doing so are a lot more complicated and nuanced than is often believed. We live in a hostile environment for trans people, so it's only natural that some may feel pressured to detransition in order to escape harm. This fear around detransitioning means increased barriers for trans people to access the healthcare they need.

The cissexism that is pervasive in our society creates structural issues that impact the wellbeing of trans people. The result is a complete lack of funding, resources and access for trans healthcare services, which means astronomical waiting lists. In the UK, at the time of writing, people who were referred in November 2017 are only now being offered their first appointment (Gender Identity Clinic, n.d.). That's over four years later.

The UK government is doing very little to rectify this situation. In 2020 Liz Truss, the Minister for Women and Equalities, announced that they would be adding three more gender clinics to reduce waiting lists by 1600 people by 2022. However, as revealed by Vic Parsons for PinkNews (2020), these were pilot schemes that were already announced and had been taking patients all summer. While this is still good news, reducing the waiting list by 1600, when the waiting list at the time of the article was 13,500, shows that the UK government is not taking the issue seriously.

Further to this, the UK government in 2020 essentially scrapped plans to reform the Gender Recognition Act, which would have made it easier for trans people to have their gender legally recognized (Stonewall, n.d.). All of this causes undue hardship to trans people, such as worse mental health issues, as previously noted.

Being m-spec and trans

While I have spoken at length about how people conflate gender identity, gender expression and sexuality, there is another conflation that is also worth discussing: the conflation between being m-spec and being trans. As Eisner breaks down in her book (2013), this stems from the idea of being 'two in one' (p.244), where trans people are seen to be both a man and a woman. Due to this transphobic notion, trans people are sometimes seen as inherently m-spec, since they can neither be gay nor straight no matter who they are attracted to. Further to this, trans people are seen as a 'bisexual threat to society since, according to transphobic thought, desiring trans people means you're secretly into "both sexes"' (p.244).

Phillip told me that when cisallo straight people know either that Phillip is trans or that they are bi, and then learn they are bi or trans respectively, these people normally aren't surprised or tell them that it 'makes sense now'. Phillip said that while they don't experience this issue now, in the early days after coming out a lot of people seemed to expect that his partner would also have to be trans and bi. A lot of people believed that cis people wouldn't want to date him and expected that his partner would need to be m-spec. This very likely stems from this conflation, that desiring trans people made you m-spec because trans people are 'both sexes'.

This conflation and what I have written up to this point seem almost at odds with one another and yet, somehow, both ideologies co-exist. This, in and of itself, shows how little transphobia makes sense. It shows the extent of ignorance and bigotry surrounding trans people, as well as m-spec people, in our society and how society's framework of cissexism and mono-sexism means that people constantly view everything through the lens of this binary.

In the LGBTQIA+ community

With all the bigotry that trans m-spec people face in society, where can they go to exist freely? The LGBTQIA+ community often isn't a space where trans m-spec men can feel safe. The next chapter focuses on the m-spec phobia and erasure that exist within the LGBTQIA+ community, but we have already seen numerous examples of this. Transphobia is also prevalent within the LGBTQIA+ community, with groups like Get The L Out being prime examples of this.

Will told me that he found LGBTQIA+ spaces to be very

cisgender focused, which made him feel both uncomfortable and excluded. Phillip also said that there were occasions where he wasn't welcomed very warmly in LGBTQIA+ spaces, which were either specifically for or heavily populated by cisallo gay men. Oliver told me that he often felt anxious in LGBTQIA+ spaces, especially when using the toilet as he had to use a stall to pee. He said that this created awkward conversations and he was often fearful of being discovered as a trans man.

Jameson said that in some LGBTQIA+ spaces, he and his husband are perceived by others to be a straight couple. This is frustrating for Jameson on multiple levels. Jameson is a non-binary trans man, so their relationship with their husband is anything but straight. Jameson is in a same-sex relationship, so to be perceived as being in a straight relationship is erasing of his gender identity. Both Jameson and his husband are m-spec, so being perceived as a straight couple and being made to feel unwelcome in LGBTQIA+ spaces is erasing of both of their sexualities.

Statistics from Stonewall (2018b) show that 36 per cent of trans people experienced discrimination within their local LGBT community. There is a clear level of hostility here and it is important that this is addressed.

M-spec and/or trans spaces

So what about spaces that specifically cater to m-spec and/or trans people? In her book, Eisner (2013) discusses the issues around transphobia in bisexual communities and biphobia in trans communities.

She states that while the bisexual community is light years ahead of other activist communities, including gay and lesbian communities, when it comes to the inclusion of trans people, there are still issues here. These issues include cissexist language (e.g. 'men and women' and 'both sexes'), lack of trans people leading groups, tokenism and more. While the commonly used definition of bisexual is 'attraction to more than one gender', we cannot ignore the usage of the definition 'attraction to men and women' used both historically and, by some (arguably many, especially those who live outside trans-inclusive communities), even presently.

Eisner mentions that her first experience of a bi community outside her own was BiCon in the UK and she was shocked by the lack of inclusion of trans people. There was very little in the way of workshops or spaces that specifically targeted trans people, leading to the feeling of being marginalized.

Eisner writes that when looking at trans communities, she finds that they are often unconcerned about bisexuality. She says that trans communities often erase bi people entirely, rejecting bisexual as a valid identity, conflating bi with lesbian and gay when discussing the exclusion of trans people and stating that bi reinforces a gender binary. In fact, the exclusion from the trans community is what prompted Eisner to undertake bi activism.

We have to remember that monosexism and cissexism are both structural issues that exist in society. Many of us are brought up in a world that rejects trans and m-spec identities. Unless we do the work to unlearn that bigotry, we may continue to perpetuate it. The result is what we have seen here, trans-phobia existing in m-spec spaces and m-spec phobia existing in trans spaces. The issue in these spaces is a product of the structures created in wider society.

Thankfully, those I spoke to had mostly positive things to say about their experiences within trans spaces. Phillip said that they had always had very pleasant experiences in the trans-specific spaces that they accessed. He found a lot of the people were also m-spec, so the space was incredibly welcoming and made him feel that all parts of his identity were accepted.

Similarly, Oliver told me that he found his local trans support group to be one of the most accepting communities he had ever met. He found that the majority of the people in this space were also m-spec or gay with very few being straight, therefore it was easy to be forthcoming about his whole identity in this space. He started as a service user but is now on the board of trustees as he wants to give back.

Not many had experiences of m-spec spaces, mainly because they were unaware of a local community. There are reasons for this which will be discussed more in the next chapter. There also didn't seem to be any awareness of spaces that catered to people who were both m-spec and trans. One person I spoke to, Hann, told me that prior to the pandemic he and another trans person were working on creating such a space as trans and non-binary m-spec people didn't always feel welcome in cis-majority meetings or events put on by the m-spec community. A space which focuses on this intersection can be incredibly helpful in tackling the specific issues this community faces.

M-spec and People of Colour (POC)

There are not many reports that research the intersectional experiences of m-spec people of colour and their issues. In order to fill this gap, Bi's of Colour created a survey to understand the struggles that this group faces (Applebee 2015). While the majority of respondents were women, it is useful to see how the issues might impact m-spec men of colour.

Many of the respondents discussed how LGBTQIA+ communities were mostly dominated by white people and tend to focus on lesbian and gay people. They discussed how they experienced racism and Islamophobia, which often made them feel excluded or isolated by the mainstream queer movement. Not only that, but they also experienced m-spec erasure within the LGBTQIA+ community, being told that they weren't actually queer or were secretly gay. One mentioned how they felt they were tokenized as they were made the POC spokesperson in asexual communities.

Outside the LGBTQIA+ community, there were various discussions on rejection from friends or from family, where it was evident that their cultural background played a part in this rejection. There was a fear of being disowned or told that they would never be accepted and find love.

This report brings a lot of talking points to light on the intersectional experience of m-spec people of colour, and even more besides. In this section, I will be delving into people's personal experiences and how they have overcome these increased barriers.

Masculinity

Growing up in a British Indian household and in an area that was predominately populated with South Asian people (Southall in West London), I found myself constantly surrounded with the expectations of what it meant to be a man.

Many South Asian cultures are steeped in heteronormativity and with this come certain expectations on how people behave, which often means enforcing strict, traditional and archaic gender roles.

For men, the expectation is to be the provider, to be strong and unemotional, to be rich and successful in order to support your wife and kids. This creates an air of toxic masculinity. As mentioned previously, masculinity is often intrinsically tied to heterosexuality in society and therefore these expectations also come with the expectation for people to be straight.

While these expectations exist in society as a whole, they are certainly more pronounced within South Asian communities and the pressure comes from the whole community to conform to these ideals. I will touch more on this shortly.

I often found myself berated for my actions, as they were seen to be feminine attributes, such as crying or playing with soft toys. This happened even within my own household, where my dad would ask when I would 'stop acting like a girl'.

I was often seen as gay and ridiculed for that by people in my own community. This was incredibly damaging as I was struggling with my identity and my attraction to genders other than the one that I was 'meant' to be attracted to (women). This meant that I hid my feelings for men as I knew it would not be accepted by my community. I felt that expressing these feelings would only intensify the cruelty I experienced and I would no longer be welcome in our spaces.

Blizzb3ar is a Black bisexual man and told me that his community is very similar in their expectations of men. He said that there is sense of hypermasculinity that runs throughout Black culture, and Black men who shy away from masculinity are frowned on. With this, LGBTQIA+ people are often shunned. Blizzb3ar said that when he came out, he did get some hate from the Black community to the point that he no longer felt comfortable in the community nor that he belonged.

Joseph, who is also a Black bisexual man, told me that LGBTQIA+ people in his community would often be asked, 'Where was your father in all this?' According to Joseph, there are two different implications in this. One is that your father was not present, that you probably grew up in a single-parent household and the lack of a strong father figure is the reason you turned out unmasculine and therefore queer. The other is potential sexual perversion. There is an almost superstitious belief that those men who turn out queer in this community were likely to have been raped or sexually assaulted by their father or a male figure, such as an uncle, in their childhood. It is believed that it was this being their first sexual encounter that changed these men and made them queer.

This seems to come back to the idea of phallocentrism, that being penetrated by a penis alters the state of a person, changes their being; that, for men, being penetrated by a penis makes them gay. This concept is used in an abhorrent way here. Instead of being supportive of someone who was potentially abused, a survivor of sexual assault, it is weaponizing that trauma. Childhood trauma is blamed for the person turning out queer and it is used to justify bigotry.

Blizzb3ar had similar experiences, with people in his community often saying that the reason LGBTQIA+ people are LGBTQIA+ is because they either hung out with their mothers too much or didn't have a good example of what it meant to be a man.

Culture of shame

Many South Asian cultures have what is referred to as a collectivist culture. 'In such cultures, relationships with other members of the group and the interconnectedness between people play a central role in each person's identity' (Cherry 2021). In many South Asian cultures, this often means that the community is very tightly knit and the perception of other people, what they think of you and your social standing within the community, is of utmost importance.

This cultivates a culture of shame. You often hear phrases like, 'Don't you have any shame?' or, 'What will people think?' This is used to encourage people to follow the unwritten rules of the community and fall in line with expectations, or else risk bringing shame on their family and ruining their social standing. Certain topics or conversations become taboo and people will hide or even lie about certain personal details in order to not create a scandal and be shamed by the community for their behaviour.

There were numerous incidents where I bore witness to the culture of shame within my community, either directly aimed at my behaviour or at those around me. One example of this which really stands out was my inability to hang out with any of my school friends who were women, mostly after school but sometimes even during school hours.

There was a concern that if they were seen with me, other people in the community might see our relationship as something sexual or romantic, rather than just the friendly relationship we held. The fear was that this would become idle gossip in the community, which would bring shame to their family, and might get back to their parents, which would create tensions in the family.

This line of thinking meant that my friends would often tell me that they couldn't hang out, or not hang out in certain areas where they might be seen by certain people prone to gossip. However, this could even come up in the school grounds, with their older brothers sometimes probing the nature of our friendship.

This culture of shame directly impacted me on numerous occasions, including when I came out. After coming out to my family, I recall my mum telling me that my dad was concerned about 'other people finding out'. They wanted me to keep my sexuality a secret, hidden. To me this felt like remaining closeted and hiding my identity.

When I told her that I would be talking publicly about my sexuality by posting in on Facebook, my mum tried to dissuade me from doing so. She questioned why I felt the need to do that, told me that it was unnecessary and nobody's business and I should just keep it to myself. This made me feel as if my sexuality was indeed something scandalous, something to be ashamed about. It followed the same pattern that is so often seen in our community.

Kamal is mixed race and while he is South Asian and the culture is quite conservative, his family have been known to push back against the norms, with the women in his family being incredibly successful and proudly feminist as far back as the 1940s and 50s.

The one thing he did notice was that his family were very much silent about LGBTQIA+ people. On a number of occasions, he was told by family members about certain LGBTQIA+ people they grew up with, but it was always in one-on-one conversations and said in hushed tones. Again, this brings us back to LGBTQIA+ identities being taboo and shameful, talked about in secret rather than something to be out and proud about.

Kamal also mentioned that he has a couple of family members who are gay but are 'allowed' to exist because they're very successful artists and nobody mentions their sexuality overtly. So it seems that to Kamal, if you're rich enough and silent enough, nobody cares.

Christianity

Kamal is also Black and said that the culture on this side of his family is incredibly homophobic, biphobic and transphobic, but he has been largely shielded from this due to his parent being estranged from his family.

He told me that the patriarchy and Christianity are very much linked to the culture and it means that the gender norms are fairly conservative and traditional, at least in theory. Kamal noted that there have been a number of transgressions from these gender norms on this side of his family, such as stay at home dads. This is partly people paying lip-service to traditionalism and religion without following it but also remnants of pre-colonial culture, where the gender power dynamic was less extreme and women played a more active part in public life.

Joseph and Blizzb3ar agreed with Kamal in that Christianity is intrinsically linked to their culture. Joseph said that instead of the 'What will others say?' that I often experienced in the British Indian community, he often heard, 'What will God think?' He said that the Bible is often brought up when people transgress the expectations of the community, in order to shame their behaviour and force them to change.

Joseph explained that has impacted his relationship with his mum, who believes that his behaviour is sinful. This attitude is hard to change as she believes that if the Bible says that it is wrong, then it's wrong and there's no changing that. Even when she is faced with information that contradicts her beliefs, she is stubborn and refuses to change her mind. This is also common in his culture, and Joseph feels that she will only change her mind if someone her age or older informs her otherwise, as his culture is also heavily steeped in 'listen to and respect your elders', which is something I see in my own community too.

Blizzb3ar had a similar experience to Joseph. Blizzb3ar told me that people in his community often put God before their family. He said that there is often a lack of compassion from the Christian community, who constantly repeat the rhetoric that being LGBTQIA+ is bad and that you're going to Hell. He noticed that people in his church would refuse to acknowledge the identity of LGBTQIA+ people, but would still condemn them for it. He would hear phrases like 'this isn't you' or 'love the sinner, hate the sin', and it almost felt as if they viewed LGBTQIA+ people as a project, where they could save them from their sin.

Blizzb3ar told me that coming out to his family didn't go well. When he first told his mum she was incredibly negative towards him. She yelled at him, called him a sinner, questioned who he was and didn't speak to him for an extended period. Eventually, she put it to the back of her mind as she thought it was all a phase and there was a chance he would end up with a woman.

In a similar way to my own community, in Blizzb3ar's community pride and image are hugely important as everyone wants to be the model family, the one everyone looks up to. He said that when he brought up his identity again, his mum asked, 'Why would you do this to me?', as if he was tarnishing the family image. Blizzb3ar lived with his family for three years after college but found himself constantly put down and unable to be himself. After coming out for the third time to his family the conversation got very heated and, as a result, he moved out of home and now barely talks to his parents. He told his parents that if he gets married and has kids, they won't be there.

Colonialization

It would be remiss of me to discuss these issues without considering the impact of colonialization.

In India, homosexuality was illegal for over 100 years. However the law, section 377, which made homosexuality illegal, was put in place by the British during their rule over India. While it didn't explicitly include the word 'homosexual', it made sexual acts that were deemed against the natural order illegal. There-fore, this law was used to criminalize and prosecute homosexual activity.

India wasn't alone in this. Various other countries, including Jamaica where Joseph's family originate from, also had similar laws, often called buggery laws, which were put in place by the British when they ruled these countries. While the British Empire is over and most if not all of these countries have gained independence from the UK, these laws are still in place and have become entrenched in the culture of the country and the community.

However, prior to these laws being placed, there is evidence that these countries were a lot more accepting of LGBTQIA+ identities. In India, there are sculptures, texts and poetry that show that same-sex attraction was seen as acceptable. Joseph told me that what little he has seen has shown this to be true in Jamaica as well. Joseph also said that he has seen documents which show that in certain civilisations in Western Africa, it used to be acceptable for two men to hold hands even as friends. In fact, an article from Stonewall (Buckle 2020) highlights how numerous African countries were accepting of LGBTQIA+ identities prior to colonialization; for example Egypt, where two men were found buried together in a lovers' embrace, or Angola, where men dressed in women's apparel.

More and more of this history is being unearthed, showing that these countries did not criminalize or villainize LGBTQIA+ identities prior to British rule. In fact, the British likely saw these sexual acts and displays of gender expression in these countries and deemed them wrong, marked the people as savages and sought to civilize them by putting down these laws.

Christianity played a huge part in this. Christianity fuelled British views on the behaviour of those in the countries they were colonizing. Same-sex acts were seen as sinful, as we have already noted, which is why they saw these people as savages for engaging in such behaviour. As the British colonized different areas of the world, they exported Christianity and sought to bring these people into God's light.

It should be noted that it was not the British alone who were responsible for colonialization and the spread of Western European Christianity. The French, Spanish and Portuguese, among others, all played a part in sending missionaries out to various countries, and each had their own empires.

So while colonial powers (e.g. the British in India) were responsible for the laws around the world that criminalized same-sex sexual acts and LGBTQIA+ identities, we cannot downplay the impact of the spread of Western European Christianity by these other powers and how it altered the views, perceptions and culture of these communities.

These views have impacted the culture of these communities greatly, including the diaspora communities. As people moved from their native country to countries in the western world, such as the UK and the US, they have brought these views over with them and this forms the bedrock of the culture of the diaspora communities. This is then reinforced by the deeply embedded structural heterosexism and heteronormativity in the UK and US.

Even as the culture in places like India, among others, shifts as they shed the laws and rules imposed by colonialization, in my personal opinion it often feels as if the culture in the diaspora has been slower to change (but of course different parts of a community can grow and change in different ways). My British Indian community often holds on to the toxic attitudes that existed within their native land when they left, refusing to critique, analyse or change their ideas. They believe that if they do so, they are letting go of their culture, losing their connection to their motherland and assimilating into whiteness.

I have often been called a coconut for straying away from what it means to be a South Asian man. Coconut is a term that means brown on the outside and white on the inside and is often used in a derogatory fashion to shame someone for their behaviours. If I indulged in anything seen to be 'other', from music to TV shows, to the way I spoke to people or dressed, it prompted people to call me a coconut – this is to say that I am not a 'proper' Indian, that I am out of touch with my culture, that I have been altered (for the worse) by being born in the UK.

This can also revolve around queerness. Joseph told me that his queerness often gets labelled as white behaviour. He said that people from his community state that they won't be able to become free because of people like him doing what the white people tell them to do. He has been labelled an Oreo as a result, meaning, similar to coconut, black on the outside and white on the inside.

It is frustrating that our communities don't seem to realize that the concept of being queer is not a white concept, but was part of our culture before white people interjected and changed it. In fact, being against LGBTQIA+ identities is upholding white supremacy.

Worse than this, these attitudes in our communities mean that white people, who have (at least in some ways) moved on from their objections to LGBTQIA+ identities, see people of colour as regressive. As places like the UK have removed their buggery laws, legalized same-sex marriage and started teaching about LGBTQIA+ identities in schools, they see themselves as progressive and other countries that are behind them in this regard as backwards.

It feels as if the savages narrative has been flipped. Where we were once labelled savages for our so-called sexual deviancy, allowing same-sex acts to occur without restriction, we are now being labelled as such for outlawing such behaviour. This misses the fact that we never technically outlawed this behaviour; it was a restriction placed on us by British rule and these countries are still trying to undo the harm of colonialization.

This is an important conversation to have. So often when we discuss the struggles LGBTQIA+ people of colour face due to the queerphobic discrimination within our own community, we don't talk about the root cause of this. This can mean we play into this narrative that people of colour are regressive or backwards. The context here is necessary to explain how this culture has been formed and the work our community is doing to try to separate our culture from the colonial mindset.

In POC communities

All of this means that many queer people of colour, such as myself, do not feel safe within their cultural community. They fear that if they were to be visibly queer in this space, they may experience discrimination.

I often feel out of place in my British Indian community. I often get looks or have people make comments about me and the way I look, my lack of masculinity. I don't think I would feel very safe being open about my bisexuality in these spaces. I have walked around Southall with my boyfriend and while I didn't experience any discrimination when I was there, I did feel somewhat on edge as I was fearful of what could happen.

Joseph told me that while he doesn't hide his identity on the occasion he attends Black, non-queer community events (often with family), he also doesn't showcase his identity in this space.

He said that he wouldn't bring his partners to this space and loudly out himself as he wouldn't feel comfortable doing so. He fears if he did, he would garner a lot of judgemental looks and people would tell him to stop or leave.

In the LGBTQIA+ community

Entering LGBTQIA+ spaces was a big step for me in owning my sexuality and identity. But I learned pretty quickly that I wouldn't be fully accepted in these spaces. LGBTQIA+ spaces are often very white dominated, and this can make them quite unsettling places for a queer person of colour such as myself.

I found that while people in this space could relate to me on some level in regard to my experiences with my sexuality, there was a lot that they didn't quite understand. They didn't get how my race played a factor in my experiences when it came to my sexuality. They didn't understand the experience of being both bi and a person of colour. I struggled with feeling seen in these spaces. It felt lonely when I didn't have people who could empathize with my situation or understand the complexities surrounding it.

Worse than this, I found that I wasn't always welcome in LGBTQIA+ spaces. I would often get looks when entering these spaces, unwelcoming ones. It felt as if I was something foreign, unexpected and unwanted.

On apps, I would see both racism and fetishization. 'No fats, no femmes, no Asians' was a common thing people would put in their profiles on apps like Grindr, along with others like 'no rice' or people looking for a 'big black cock'. These sorts of comments made me feel objectified and commodified, and gave me a feeling of being unsafe in these spaces. And I know I'm not alone in feeling like this.

I also realized that my views were unwelcome in LGBTQIA+ spaces. I found I could no longer bring up topics around race without people trying to silence me. Topics such as institutional racism, cultural appropriation and reverse racism were often met with defensiveness, criticism, white fragility and silencing.

Joseph also experienced issues in the LGBTQIA+ community. He often found himself fetishized, both in person and on dating and hook-up apps. He saw people seeking a 'big black cock' or 'BBC' as it is often known, and was even asked outright if he had one. He found that people saw him as masculine, dominant and aggressive because of his Blackness, and fetishized that.

Blizzb3ar experienced similar issues on apps such as Grindr. He told me that in the LGBTQIA+ community, white people were often favoured and this damaged his self-esteem as he didn't see himself as preferable. When he did get attention on Grindr, he often felt as if it was his only opportunity, but these were often cases of fetishization. He, like Joseph, also experienced instances of people asking if he had a 'BBC' or 'big Black cock' and once got a message where someone said 'Give me that monkey cock'. Blizzb3ar told me that Grindr and similar apps ruined his mental health and if he could go back, he would have stopped himself from using them.

This issue isn't only present in the LGBTQIA+ community. Joseph experienced this from cisallohet people too, especially white cisallohet women. There are women who call themselves 'Queen of Spades' and sometimes get this, or a black spade, tattooed on them. These are women who sleep exclusively with Black men, even when they have a husband who is white or non-Black. They call the Black men 'bulls', to define them as the alpha male.

This whole subculture is extremely fetishizing, incredibly objectifying and rooted in racism and anti-Blackness. While these issues aren't restricted to the LGBTQIA+ community alone, it shows that the LGBTQIA+ community is just a microcosm of society as a whole. Racism doesn't disappear just because the community is marginalized. White LGBTQIA+ people are still white and can and do uphold racism and white supremacy.

In fact, statistics from Stonewall (2018) show that 51 per cent of LGBT people of colour experienced racism within their local LGBT community. And when looking specifically at Black people, 61 per cent of Black LGBT people experienced racism in their local LGBT community.

Being M-spec and POC

It is clear that LGBTQIA+ people of colour face unique challenges due to their multiple marginalized identities. Being LGBTQIA+ in your cultural community is difficult as it isn't always accepting of your identity. You may feel uncomfortable in this space and feel you can't be yourself without being shamed to change.

Meanwhile, being a person of colour in the LGBTQIA+ community means you may experience racism, just as you would in the wider society, due to how white dominated these spaces are. This can come in many forms, from exclusion and microaggressions to a lack of understanding and downplaying of your experiences as a person of colour, and even being fetishized. This happens not just on an interpersonal level, but on a structural level, where LGBTQIA+ people of colour are harassed, abused and excluded, meaning they are unable to access community resources and create change.

But what are the unique challenges of being an m-spec man and a person of colour? As mentioned previously, m-spec men can be fetishized within the LGBTQIA+ community due to their perceived masculinity. Black men also experience this and so the fetishization that Black m-spec men experience can be intensified.

There are also issues around sexual health. Black m-spec men are often demonized, seen to be hiding their identity, as being 'on the down low'. Joseph told me how Black m-spec men within the Black community are seen as carriers for disease, namely HIV but also other STDs, and therefore seen as a risk factor to the rest of the Black community. He recalled how after coming out to his family, one of his brothers said that he 'didn't want to speculate about the diseases' Joseph had.

There can be a certain pressure to conform to a heteronormative life, which isn't unique to m-spec people of colour but can certainly be more pronounced. I found that when I came out, my mum partly saw it as a relief. She told me that since I was still attracted to women, I could simply get into a relationship with a woman, have kids and so on. Essentially, I could still live the heteronormative life they desired from me. It felt like, to them, my identity didn't matter. If I could get into a relationship with a woman, then they could forget all about my identity.

Having to contend with both m-spec phobia and racism at the same time can make life incredibly difficult. LGBTQIA+ spaces are rife with both, so when you aren't dealing with racism, you may be dealing with m-spec phobia or erasure, making it hard to exist safely in this space.

Spaces catering for m-spec people have the same problem of often being white dominated, meaning that while you may be free from the m-spec phobia, you may still experience racism. Bi's of Colour, which I referenced in my introduction to this section, was born out of the racism they saw in m-spec spaces. In an essay entitled 'Bisexuals of Color', Applebee (2018) writes of their experience at BiCon 2009, one of the biggest events for m-spec people in the UK, and the racism they witnessed. One of the organizers used racist slurs and after being told to stop, they played victim.

After this, Applebee organized a session solely for bi people of colour at the next BiCon in 2010. Those who attended the session found it incredibly healing in many ways, but there were complaints from delegates that bis of colour shouldn't have their own separate session as BiCon was friendly to everyone. This prompted Applebee to point out how few people of colour were in attendance at BiCon.

Meanwhile, spaces made for queer people of colour may be free of racism, but may still be rife with m-spec phobia and erasure. I personally have been in queer people of colour spaces and seen and experienced m-spec erasure and m-spec phobia. I have been called greedy and witnessed m-spec public figures be consistently erased. Joseph told me how he had people see him as 'down low' even in queer people of colour spaces.

Impact

This highlights the difficulty of being an m-spec person of colour. Having to grapple with your sexual identity and your cultural identity at the same time can be a struggle. You have to contend simultaneously with both racism and queerphobia, and in spaces where others would find safety, you find more bigotry. Finding a space to exist as your whole self can be nearly impossible and this can be incredibly damaging.

The impact this can have on your mental health should not be understated. There aren't any statistics that show the specific issues of m-spec people of colour, let alone m-spec men of colour. But when statistics show that m-spec men are more likely to struggle with their mental health, and there are similar statistics for people of colour, you can draw your own conclusions on the difficulties faced by m-spec men of colour. And much the same can be said when it comes to the sexual health of m-spec men of colour.

Being shut out of spaces from multiple different angles means it's hard to gain access to the resources you need, find the network of support you need and connect with like-minded people who understand your specific issues. There are increased barriers to health services, as we have already seen, and dating becomes a minefield.

However, change is happening. The m-spec community, at least here in the UK, has taken note of the problems within the community. It has spent time, energy and money on being anti-racist and doing more to support m-spec people of colour, give them a platform, create a safe space for them, and give them a voice.

While there are issues, numerous people spoke about how they feel more at ease within LGBTQIA+ spaces, especially ones dominated or created by queer people of colour, and how they have been able to embrace their full selves in these spaces.

M-spec and A-spec

A-spec people are people who are on the asexual spectrum (ace-spec) or the arosexual spectrum (aro-spec) or both. People who are both m-spec and a-spec are described as cross-orientated, which means their romantic orientation and sexual orientation don't align. As mentioned earlier, most people believe these two to be one and the same. So, for example, bisexual people are seen as those who are romantically and sexually attracted to more than one gender. However, this isn't always the case. You could be someone who is romantically attracted to more than one gender, for example, but experience little to no sexual attraction to any gender whatsoever. If so, you may identify as biromantic asexual.

In this section, I will discuss those who are both m-spec and a-spec and how the stereotypes and assumptions for these two communities sometimes conflict, meaning people who are both experience discrimination from both ends. And in some cases, they can align, meaning the bigotry can worsen. I will discuss the discrimination experienced by a-spec people, people who are on the asexual or aromatic spectrum, who are also m-spec. I will highlight the similarities and differences, and show how this can impact people who belong to both communities.

Allonormativity

Discrimination towards ace-spec people – people on the asexual spectrum – has some similarities to that experienced by m-spec people. One of the common things ace-spec people hear is that they're confused or just going through a phase (OULGBTQ+ Society, n.d.). For m-spec people, as previously mentioned, this idea stems from monosexism, which is the belief that only monosexual identities (gay or straight) are real (Eisner 2013). For ace-spec people, the issue they often have to grapple with is allonormativity (Ferguson 2019).

Allosexual is the opposite term to asexual and describes people who do experience sexual attraction. Allonormativity is a term used to describe the societal belief that all people experience sexual attraction and that sex and sexual attraction are a normal part of the human experience.

However, this is not necessarily the case for people who sit on the asexual spectrum. Some may never experience sexual attraction or may only experience it after a romantic bond has been formed. Some may be sex repulsed or have no desire for a sexual relationship. There are a number of ways this can present itself.

But society believes that allosexuality is the norm. Allonormativity stems from allosexism which, in a similar vein to monosexism, is the structural privileging of allosexual behaviour (Abrams 2019). This leads to the erasure of ace-spec identities and gives rise to acephobia, which is discrimination that targets people on the asexual spectrum.

Liam came out to his parents as asexual at 13. He experienced backlash on doing so, being told that he wasn't actually asexual and that you 'can't have a meaningful relationship without sex'. This is an example of the allonormative mindset that exists in society and the acephobia that those who sit outside this norm experience as a result.

Due to this experience and Liam's desire to have a 'meaningful relationship', Liam questioned his identity and spent years bouncing between different identities to find one that fitted, one that made sense with his feelings. Liam is also trans and biromantic and started accessing therapy at 12, when he came out as a trans guy, in order to be diagnosed with gender dysphoria so he could access gender-affirming healthcare.

However, a couple of years later, he started seeing a therapist to help him deal with his depression and anxiety. Part of Liam's struggles with his mental health stemmed from his identity. He found that he constantly doubted himself and convinced himself that he needed to experience sexual attraction. He thought something might change and maybe it would happen when he started taking testosterone or when he met the right person.

When it didn't happen, it impacted Liam greatly. It made him feel as if he was doing something wrong, that he was broken and defective. These thoughts and feelings were already present due to his struggles with his gender identity and mental health issues, so this only exacerbated the issue.

Further to this, Liam also struggled with his romantic identity. He found himself attracted to women and non-binary people but wasn't sure what label to use. Liam thought that bi meant attraction to men and women, but since he wasn't attracted to men, he didn't think this label was right. But trying other labels, such as straight, didn't seem to work for him either.

Despite expressing his identity as biromantic asexual at 13, Liam spent years struggling with his identity and being confused over who he was, only to reach the same conclusion seven years later. He believed that what his parents said was true, so much so that he struggled to come to terms with the fact that it wasn't and his parents were simply invalidating him and his identity.

Amatonormativity

Aro-spec people – people on the aromantic spectrum – also have to deal with the stereotype that their identity is 'just a phase' (OULGBTQ+ Society, n.d.). In this case, the main factor is amatonormativity. Amatonormativity is a term used to describe the societal belief that everyone wants a romantic relationship and that romantic love is prioritized over other kinds of love (Barker, n.d.; Brake, n.d.). It is the idea that the norm is to be alloromantic, which is the opposite of aromantic and means that you experience romantic attraction (Ferguson 2019). Due to this, people on the aromantic spectrum are often erased or experience discrimination, called arophobia.

Roe told me that they grew up in a very evangelical town, which was extremely amatonormative. They grew up being taught abstinence-based sex education and had to do purity pledges, promising not to have sex until marriage. This made Roe feel as if they were experiencing attraction in the wrong way due to their lack of romantic attraction. They were taught that the way you show someone you care is with romance and making a commitment to your partner.

This meant that Roe often forced themselves into romantic relationships and performing romance in order to please their partner. They struggled with this massively as they weren't sure what to do in order to fulfil the romantic expectations of a relationship and often relied on movie tropes and using their ex-partners' critiques as lessons. This made them miserable.

As Roe entered college, they decided to go into psychology. In the introductory module of this course, they covered attachment styles. The behaviours associated with the avoidant attachment style, such as partners labelling you distant, feeling uncomfortable when partners get emotionally close and so on, seemed to fit Roe's experiences of relationships.

This hurt Roe deeply and confirmed for them what various partners had previously said, that there was something wrong with them, that they were broken and needed to be fixed. They were taught that being unable to have long-term committed relationships was a sign of poor mental health and so they believed that their relationship preferences were due to their trauma disorder and the hypersexuality they experienced when they were hypomanic.

This prompted Roe to try to fix themselves, forcing themselves to stick it out in very poor relationships and often blaming themselves for the toxic nature of the relationship.

As we can see, monosexism, allosexism and amatonormativity

can have a profound impact on people. The structural privileging of monosexual, allosexual and allormantic identities means that education on m-spec, ace-spec and aro-spec identities is sorely lacking. This leads to a society that is rife with m-spec phobia, arophobia and acephobia and erasure that can be internalized, causing people to struggle with their identity, which can greatly impact their mental health.

This can be seen with Liam, who internalized the acephobia and invalidation he experienced from his parents. He also struggled with the use of biromantic to describe his attraction to women and non-binary people. The lack of education about the spectrum of m-spec identities and the different ways they can present could be one of the factors here. Liam mentioned how the curriculum was lacking when it came to LGBTQIA+ issues, and support from teachers was inconsistent, as there appeared to be no training in LGBTQIA+ identities and limited understanding.

The split attraction model

Monosexism, allosexism and amatonormativity impact m-spec, ace-spec and aro-spec people respectively. But those who are both m-spec and a-spec experience these issues simultaneously and a new challenge presents itself.

Society often does not acknowledge the existence of the split attraction model, which is the idea that sexual orientation and romantic orientation are two different things that may or may not necessarily align (The Asexual Visibility & Education Network, n.d.). The dismissal of this model to describe attraction means that those who are cross-orientated or variorientated (Western Aces, n.d.) are erased.

This is referred to as periorientism (Arco-Pluris, n.d.) – where someone's sexual attraction and romantic attraction align. For example, someone who is attracted both sexually and romantically to more than one gender is both biromantic and bisexual. However, people often use one term to describe both sides of their attraction, so they may just use bisexual.

The romantic element is often not described as they are assumed to be one and the same. Periorientism, in a similar vein to monosexism and allosexism, involves the structural privileging of periorientated people and the belief that everyone should be periorientated. This leads to variphobia, which is the discrimination against cross-orientated people.

Naturally, lack of education plays a role here yet again. Drew mentioned how they grew up under section 28, so naturally they didn't learn a single thing about queer identities or sexuality. For Jupiter, sexual education in school really pushed the idea that once you hit puberty, you start to experience sexual attraction to people and sexual attraction is normal, but there wasn't any mention of people who don't experience sexual or romantic attraction. They said that they didn't know it was a possibility to grow up and not experience sexual or romantic attraction and were unaware of asexuality and romanticism.

As mentioned earlier, Roe was given abstinence-based sex education, which came with the idea that sex was something for committed relationships. This enforced the idea that you had to form romantic relationships, which wasn't something Roe desired. Their college degree in psychology also made them believe that their lack of romantic attraction was due to poor mental health.

This lack of education on a-spec and m-spec identities naturally means that there was a lack of understanding about being cross-orientated. Some of the people I spoke to were aware of m-spec and/or a-spec terms when they were experiencing certain feelings that made them question their identity, but this was mostly found through the internet or friends who had come out as such. The school system had failed almost everyone I spoke to, with no information or support.

The stereotypes of m-spec people can conflict with the stereotypes of a-spec people, which can create confusion about how someone can have both identities at once, and this can be internalized. For example, as mentioned previously, m-spec people are often seen as hypersexual, which juxtaposes the stereotype that all ace-spec people are virgins (OULGBTQ+ Society, n.d.).

Drew told me how they are neither and that this stereotyping can seem contradictory at times. They said that internally there's a slight disjunction, as they find themselves thinking someone is hot but at the same time they have no feelings beyond that initial wow and no desire to do anything. Alexander also mentioned this, saying that often people think that they either want to date everyone or date no one, that they are either a slut or a prude.

On the other hand, the stereotypes of being a-spec and m-spec can play off one another and exacerbate the discrimination that one may receive. Roe told me how they feel they can never escape the promiscuous m-spec trope. In high school, it was well known among their peers that they had slept with both boys and girls. Because of this, combined with the fact that they couldn't convincingly date anyone, they were labelled a slut. They were seen as always down for sex, and the handful of lesbian and gay people saw them as confused or predatory. Because they have and desire sexual relationships with people of different genders and the fact that they will never find themselves in a long-term monogamous relationship, people will continue to label them as promiscuous.

Being cross-orientated

Drew told me that due to being cross-orientated, their journey to coming out was a lot harder and more confusing than it otherwise might have been if they were periorientated. They experienced attraction to more than one gender around the ages of nine and ten, but didn't recognize those feelings as what they actually were. Around 12–13 they realized they didn't experience sexual attraction in the same way as everyone else, as everyone around them went crazy over the latest celebrity or pin-up.

But they didn't come out until they were 37. Despite learning about m-spec terms when they were 15, they had ruled out this identity as they lacked interest in having sex. They learned about asexuality when they were 26, but they didn't think the term fitted them as they got horny and had some limited attraction. Their lack of knowledge about the asexual spectrum and the split attraction model held them back.

When they learned about demisexuality, they found that things started to click into place. They slowly started to understand why they found people attractive but had no interest in doing anything with them.

If they had known about the split attraction model previously, they could have reconciled their interest in more than one gender as romantically based and found it easier to express their feelings and lack of interest in sex. But due to periorientism, this knowledge was not available and held Drew back from understanding themselves and coming out as biromatic/panromantic demisexual/greyasexual.

Drew often found themselves invalidated by people, being told that bi people couldn't be ace and that ace people were just straight people looking for attention.

Roe often found themselves invalidated too as people didn't

understand how someone could be both bisexual and aromantic. Roe found that people often used their lack of romantic attraction in order to invalidate their bisexual identity, stating that if Roe was really into a certain gender, then they would romantically date them.

Jupiter is both asexual and demibiromantic and finds that people often don't understand what this means. Many seem to think that they desire or need a romantic relationship due to being biromantic, not understanding that since they are demibiromantic, they therefore rarely experience romantic attraction. He often struggles with friendships as people think that he's interested in the other person when he never is. Jupiter is more platonically attracted and desires strong friendships.

There is an internal struggle that comes with this. Jupiter sometimes finds it hard to interpret whether they are romantically attracted to someone or not because while it is rare, it can happen, since they are demibiromantic and are attracted to all genders. However, they find that they can't communicate this to other people as others just read it as romantic attraction.

Alexander also finds that the reaction to their identity can change when someone only knows part of their identity and then finds out the rest. Alexander said that when people know he is bi, and then he comes out as ace, people think he is broken or depressed. But when people know he is ace and then he comes out as bi, people think he is indecisive or was lying about being ace.

Coming out as both ace-spec and m-spec is often met with derision. Alexander told me that he sees a lot of commentary on cross-orientated people being indecisive or special snowflakes, which he finds incredibly frustrating. He likes using multiple labels as it helps him describe himself and what goes on in his head clearly to other people and it drives him up the wall that people think he is just trying to be special.

Alexander said that they find themselves being less open about their identity as a result. They have found themselves mocked on numerous occasions for being too complicated and it's exhausting. They will tell people if they ask directly but they don't bother correcting people who think they are 'just bisexual'.

Impact

The impact of the structure of periorientism, monosexism, allosexism and amatonormativity can be huge. It means that people, like Drew, are unable to figure out their identity fully and it makes it harder to come out. It means that people, like Roe, go back in the closet in order to perform to societal expectations. It means that people, like Alexander, hide their identity in order to avoid bigotry. It can make it hard to form the bonds you want with people, whether they be platonic, sexual or romantic, due to the lack of societal understanding and the discrimination you receive.

This can all impact people's mental health. Roe told me that going back in the closet early in college did a number on their mental health, causing their bipolar to get out of hand and lead to them being diagnosed.

But getting the help and support you need isn't always easy. As mentioned in the chapter on health, costs and waiting times as well as mental health stigma can be huge obstacles to accessing support. And even after getting over those hurdles, you still may not get the right level of support.

Some may feel unable to come out to health professionals, like Roe who chose not to disclose their identities to any psychiatrist, as they knew how they would be viewed due to what they learned in their degree. Others may experience discrimination, like Alexander, who found their asexual identity questioned by the therapist and wondered whether there was a part of them that was unable to consent to sex.

Accessing spaces

Accessing LGBTQIA+ spaces is not easy either. Roe told me that they found LGBTQIA+ communities quite hostile. They said that they often saw m-spec phobia and that a-spec people were rarely included. They mentioned that the amatonormativity in LGBTQIA+ spaces, especially those dominated by lesbian and gay people, is quite strong and there is often an air of suspicion around those who are not interested in romantic relationships as they are seen as ashamed of their identity or closeted.

Jupiter said that online LGBTQIA+ communities are similar, where people often claim that a-spec people aren't really queer and just trying to claim oppression. He's also seen similar conversations around m-spec people, claiming that they have 'straight passing privilege'.

Finding spaces which cater to m-spec people or a-spec people was a mixed bag. Some of the people I asked hadn't really looked as they weren't sure if the spaces would really cater to their multiple identities. Others had found spaces, but these seemed to be mostly online. Some of these spaces were welcoming, but also had their issues.

Jupiter said that they have found some spaces online that are a lot more inclusive than in-person spaces. But, they said, they have been in some ace-spec spaces that were quite arophobic. Roe also said that the a-spec spaces tend to be more ace-centric but there are some aro-specific ones too. Alexander had been able to access m-spec and a-spec spaces in person and has found them to be broadly supportive of cross-orientated people.

As we saw with the previous sections on m-spec and POC and m-spec and trans, there were some issues in spaces that only catered to one of their identities, making it even harder to find a space. It is possible that there may be a similar issue in this case too, but thankfully the people I spoke to did not experience such issues. It does appear that finding these spaces isn't easy, however, and spaces that focus on people who belong to both communities appear non-existent.

The Importance of Intersectionality

Throughout this chapter, we have seen the experience of m-spec men who hold other marginalized identities. It is incredibly important that when we discuss the issues that m-spec people face, we ensure we do so through an intersectional lens. The other identities that people hold can make their journey with their sexuality so much more difficult. And likewise, their m-spec identity can create issues for their other identities. People who live in this liminal space have to grapple with entirely new issues that those who only sit in one space may never experience.

I have only discussed three different intersections here, but there are countless other identities that could, and should, be explored. In an article for PinkNews, Jackson King wrote about how medical fatphobia creates added stress and difficulty for trans people trying to access gender-affirming surgery (King 2021).

In an article for *Shameless* magazine, Lucinda Thee writes about the struggle of being autistic and queer. They say that people 'assume that all autistic people lack the self-awareness or judgement to identify as queer', that their desires are part of their autism and their queerness is a phase (Thee 2021). In a blog for Nono Cocoa, Karl Knights writes about how his university LGBT+ society would meet somewhere that wasn't physically accessible, and numerous other instances of ableism (Knights, n.d.).

As mentioned in the introduction to this book, some of the people I spoke to don't exclusively identify as men, if at all. Non-binary people, genderfluid people and people who identify as something other than a man or woman are often erased and forced into the gender binary. This is often done based on the gender presentation and the way the person is perceived. The way in which non-binary m-spec people are doubly erased, and the impact of this, is something that bears further discussion and is so often overlooked when discussing the issues of m-spec people and trans people.

There are countless other identities that we can discuss here, for example how class status might impact someone's ability to enter spaces due to lack of funds. Or how someone being a refugee means they risk deportation if they can't prove their sexuality to gain asylum in the UK.

Someone's sexuality is just one small part of their identity. There is so much that makes an individual who they are. It is important that we examine every part of people's identities and the way they play into one another. These other identities can play a role in the information and education they receive, the barriers they face in coming out or accessing spaces, the resources they can access, the healthcare they receive and so much more.

If we focus solely on solving the issues m-spec people as a whole face, we will miss the issues faced by those who hold other identities. Can we really say m-spec people are free if we haven't solved the way their sexuality impacts their access to gender-affirming healthcare? Can we really say m-spec people are free if physically disabled people cannot access LGBTQIA+ spaces? We need to break down the struggles of those who hold multiple marginalized identities so we can fight for their specific needs, ensure that the spaces we have are inclusive and that these people are supported in their journey. Because none of us are free until we are all free.

CHAPTER 6

Pride

Pride is a well-known, albeit somewhat overloaded, term in the LGBTQIA+ community. Pride is a term LGBTQIA+ people use on an individual level to express their feelings of self-confidence and to embrace their identity. It is also used for the physical events that are held across the world annually. However, both of these are made more difficult for m-spec people.

According to Stonewall (2018), 18 per cent of bi men have experienced discrimination based on their sexuality in LGBT spaces, compared to 4 per cent of gay men. We have seen some of these experiences in previous chapters of this book. It is clear that these so-called safe spaces that the LGBTQIA+ community have created are not safe for everyone within the community. So Pride, the pinnacle event in the LGBTQIA+ calendar and a large 'safe space', may not provide safety for everyone.

This discrimination from within the LGBTQIA+ community can cause a lot of pain. In fact, it was seen that while m-spec people experience more discrimination from heterosexual people, the relative impact of that compared to the discrimination from gay and lesbian people was the same (Greenesmith 2018).

Imagine being a newly out m-spec man wanting to connect with like-minded people and form bonds, only to find you experience the same discrimination and intolerance from the LGBTQIA+ community as from the cisallohet community.

In fact, this discrimination may be the reason why 50 per cent of bi men said that they never attend LGBT specific events and venues (Stonewall 2018). The m-spec phobia and erasure within LGBTQIA+ spaces make m-spec people feel unsafe and unwelcome, which causes them to avoid these spaces entirely.

This means that m-spec men are cut off from the community that is supposed to help them. They cannot access resources, build networks, form bonds and find support in the same way that other groups in the LGBTQIA+ community can. This has led to m-spec people creating their own spaces and own communities that work for people like them.

However, this is where a new problem arises: m-spec communities don't get any funding. According to Huffpost, 'the total amount given from foundations for bi-specific grants in 2009 and 2010 (the last two years of available data) was $0' (Andre 2012). This hasn't changed a lot since as according to the Global Resources report for 2017–2018, bisexual communities received less than 1 per cent of the funding when looking outside the US (Global Resources Report 2020).

Of course, plenty of money is going to groups that supposedly include bisexual and m-spec men or m-spec people in general, but are these spaces really including us in any meaningful way? Are they providing any support for the m-spec men who exist within their spaces? Are m-spec men even attending these groups? Are they benefitting in any way?

Without proper, well-funded spaces for m-spec men, the idea of finding pride in your sexuality becomes more difficult than it should be. The lack of community support, of connecting with like-minded people, hinders the journey of self-acceptance. In this chapter, we will unpack this issue. We will highlight further the issues that m-spec men face within LGBTQIA+ communities, spaces which they find safety in and how they journey to self-acceptance and pride within themselves.

LGBTQIA+ history

The LGBTQIA+ community has changed a lot in the last few decades; in fact, historically speaking, it often wasn't known as the LGBTQIA+ community. From events to activism groups, physical spaces and support networks, you can see that our community was often known as 'gay' or 'lesbian and gay'. The Gay Liberation Front, the March On Washington for Lesbian and Gay Rights, the London Lesbian and Gay Centre, the London Lesbian and Gay Switchboard, Gay Pride Carnival and countless other spaces, groups and events were created during the 1960s, 70s and 80s.

M-spec people were prominent in their ranks, not just as attendees but also as organizers and even founders of such spaces. As Shearing writes in their book Bi the Way (2021), m-spec activists such as Brenda Howard, ABilly Jones-Hennin and Donny the Punk played pivotal roles in helping to carve out safe spaces and fight for the rights of LGBTQIA+ people. But they weren't always accepted in these spaces.

London Lesbian and Gay Centre

In the 1980s, the London Lesbian and Gay Centre (LL&GC) decided to ban bisexual groups from their centre. In an article in issue 8 of Bi-Monthly magazine in April 1985, David Smith (1985) says that 'according to the information we have received, the Management Committee was swayed by women members who expressed the view that bisexual men were likely to harass lesbians in the Centre and their presence was not desirable' (p.2).

Of course, we cannot say that no bisexual or m-spec man may act in such a way. It is important to remember that m-spec men are still men and it is understandable why lesbians may fear a certain type of harassment or abuse from men who are attracted to women. However, to tar a whole community with the same brush and to shut out those who deserve access to such a space on these grounds is wholly unacceptable. It is also being blind to the fact that this kind of harassment and abuse can come from other avenues, such as misogynistic gay men or their fellow lesbians.

It is clear that m-spec men were seen as a risk factor to the safety of lesbians within the centre, which resulted in the ban; however, the whole situation was much murkier than this and highlights the m-spec phobia and erasure in these spaces.

In issue 9 of *Bi-Monthly* magazine, this topic is discussed again (Bi-Monthly 1985). The London Bisexual Group met with the Committee of London Lesbian and Gay Centre to discuss the ban. During this meeting, all of the objections were dismissed. Why? Because of the great semantic problem: 'bisexual people can not be "lesbian and gay"' (p.3).

They stated that the space was 'for lesbian and gay people to feel free from any pressures imposed by heterosexual society outside' (p.3). Further to this, they mentioned that the ban may be 'reconsidered if bisexual groups were to change their names to lesbian/gay bisexual groups' (p.3). It was also noted that 'one of the main objections to bisexual groups was that they had members who identified as heterosexual' and the 'most heartfelt objections' came from lesbians who objected to 'the presence of bisexual men whom they see as heterosexual and a threat' (p.3).

What this shows is that there was a significant proportion of lesbian and gay people within the LL&GC who saw m-spec people as either straight or not queer enough and therefore shouldn't be allowed access to their space.

This also brings into question the objections from lesbians. Do they view m-spec men as a threat to their safety? Or do they view m-spec men as straight and believe straight men in their space are a threat? Of course, as mentioned, this isn't to say m-spec men are somehow incapable of harassing women and making an unsafe environment, but it is interesting to analyse where lesbians believe the threat lies.

Identity as a choice

As mentioned previously in the chapter on coming out, m-spec people can sometimes be seen as able to choose to be straight. This so-called choice that m-spec identities present makes m-spec people a 'risk factor' in the eyes of lesbian and gay people and damaging to their movement.

Shearing discusses this in her book, Bi the Way (2021), stating that 'bisexuality also threatens what is called the "immutability defence" when fighting against institutional homophobia' (p.139). This is the argument that gay and lesbian people are 'born this way', that their sexuality is something innate and unchangeable. But 'bisexuals are seen as being able to choose or just be or act straight' (p.139).

There is a fear that by acknowledging the existence of m-spec people, you open the door for the argument that queer people can change their attraction and that can lead to harmful ideas like conversion therapy. Therefore m-spec people are seen as a risk factor to the cause, the movement to fight for the rights and protections of lesbian and gay people.

Shearing says that while the 'born this way' argument has done a lot of good for LGBTQIA+ rights, it also leaves a lot of 'queer people out in the cold' (p.64). It doesn't allow for the fluidity of sexuality, that the sexuality of an individual could morph and change over time. Some people identifying as lesbian or gay may later come out as m-spec, and the opposite could also be true.

Further to this, Rust (1995) says by making sexuality an essential characteristic, you open the door to the possibility of a bisexual essence. The result of this is that people identifying as lesbian or gay may have an m-spec essence and there is no way to disprove that. This could result in a reduction in the number of lesbian and gay people. But this should not be seen as a negative thing.

In a society that works in binaries, m-spec identities are often erased. This can result in people being unaware of m-spec labels and unable to see the validity in these identities. However, as people gain new knowledge about themselves as well as the world around them and the options available to them, they may redefine their identity to something they think fits them better. Identity is not something that is ever set in stone; it can grow and change as you move through the world.

We should be celebrating the fact that people have found themselves and are able to use a label that better defines who they are, rather than villainizing them for changing their identity. We must understand that the structures in our society can prevent people from using a label that better describes them and we must embrace fluidity in our identity.

Copping out

In issue 8 of Bi-Monthly magazine where the ban of bisexual groups from the LL&GC is discussed, there is also mention of the complaints that the centre had been receiving, such as 'there were suspicions that people who identified as "bisexual" were often just copping out' (Smith 1985, p.2).

Bi History, an Instagram page that shares images and information on history that involves bisexual and m-spec people, shared an image from the Queen's Crescent Club in Glasgow, which was run by the Scottish Homosexual Rights Group (Bi History 2018). In this image, we can see that on 25 February 1981, they planned an event called 'Discussion — On bisexuality. "Trend or Cop-out?"'

Stone (1996) mentions in her essay that at the Lesbian Conference in Toronto in 1979, there was a workshop dedicated to bisexuality. This included discussion of topics such as why women choose to be bisexual, whether bisexuality is a cop-out and whether bisexual women were welcome in their space.

Time and time again we can see that throughout history, bisexual and m-spec people have been erased by people in our own community. We were seen as copping out of admitting our true identity (gay/lesbian), of fully embracing our queer identity – or we were seen as actually straight and unwelcome in spaces as a result.

These are just a few examples of the abuse m-spec people receive within the community, but they are not isolated incidents. This is a systemic issue that runs deep in our community, even to this day.

Modern-day experiences

While the community may have changed over the years, becoming ever more inclusive and expansive, these attitudes still exist and are systemic in the LGBTQIA+ community. We have already seen countless examples of this within the chapters so far. From Xy being abused in an LGBTQIA+ bar they worked at to Bobby experiencing abuse on apps, we can see the same old rhetoric repeated to m-spec people in the present day.

I personally have been quizzed on my identity, asked about my previous experiences, been probed on my preferences and so much more by gay men in LGBTQIA+ spaces. One experience that comes to mind is where during a conversation I was having with a fellow bisexual man in which I disclosed my complete lack of experience with women, a gay man who overheard interrupted to ask how I knew I was bisexual and then began asking questions and casting doubt on my sexuality. No explanation seemed to quell this line of questioning and with that, I chose to no longer engage.

Levi told me that when he attended LGBTQIA+ events and parties at college, he found that people he considered his friends would introduce him to others as gay despite him telling them he identified as queer. He said this happened on numerous occasions. This made him feel inadequate and eventually he started to use gay himself in order to make other people feel comfortable.

K told me that in LGBTQIA+ spaces, people often refused to believe that he was bisexual because of the fact that he mostly dated men. This happened in physical LGBTQIA+ spaces but was more prevalent on apps like Grindr.

Gatekeeping

One thing I often see, both in person and online, is gatekeeping LGBTQIA+ events and venues. An all too common discourse seen online is the 'No straights at Pride'. Alongside this I have seen discussions on whether straight people should be allowed to attend LGBTQIA+ venues, with numerous people taking a stand against straight people going to LGBTQIA+ venues.

While this is likely to mean cisallohet people who are not part of the LGBTQIA+ community, this statement in and of itself lacks nuance. There are m-spec people, a-spec people, trans, non-binary and intersex people in the LGBTQIA+ community who may be in what people perceive to be a 'straight' relationship. But that doesn't mean that they are not part of the LGBTQIA+ community.

This often leads to hostility in real life that can make m-spec people feel unwelcome in LGBTQIA+ spaces. I have often seen people point out random couples who they perceive to be a man and a woman and talk deridingly about the straights being in our space. I have corrected people numerous times on this, both in person and online. While there is every potential that they could be straight, and there are plenty of straight people who use LGBTQIA+ spaces as their playground and take up space, assuming this can be dangerous.

I also question how you can tell someone is straight. There are no discernible features on a person that can indicate their orientation. What this often demands is that people conform to certain stereotypes of what it means to be queer. In media, this is often referred to as queer coding, where the person is never explicitly referred to as queer but the identity is hinted at through certain traits. One example of this for men is showing feminine traits through the way you talk, walk or dress.

This seems like an incredibly bizarre demand to me. Instead of 'be your authentic self', a phrase often used within the LGBTQIA+ community, we're asking people to obey certain stereotypes. It is taking that implicit inversion theory to the next level. Instead of thinking 'if a man is gay, he must be feminine' and vice versa, it is almost demanding this behaviour from people. The queer coded concept is also very much entrenched in whiteness. There is certain religious and cultural clothing that would not be seen as queer, as well as certain interests, tastes and mannerisms.

What this all amounts to is gatekeeping. It shuts people out of our community based on crude criteria, which can lead to vulnerable people without a space to be themselves. Now, I am under no illusion here. I know that there are certain groups of cisallohet people who do enter LGBTQIA+ spaces, take up space and make it unsafe for those the spaces were made for. But I believe that a much better approach is to set ground rules for the attitudes and behaviours that are expected of those within the space and remove those who cross the line. We can allow cisallohet people in the space while reminding them who the space was created by and who it is for, informing them of the rules they must abide by and telling them to not take up space for those who need it. This can also allow those who are questioning their identity access to the community without the feeling that they are not welcome.

Double discrimination

While I have spent this chapter showcasing the m-spec phobia and erasure that is prevalent in the LGBTQIA+ community, I need to make something clear. I do not believe that the LGBTQIA+ community is the source of this bigotry, nor the worst perpetrator of it. I do not believe that lesbian and gay people are the oppressors of m-spec people.

When discussing monosexism and the subsequent privilege of those who are monosexual, I am not saying that lesbian and gay people hold the same level of power as cisallohet people, nor that lesbian and gay people are not oppressed. What I am trying to show here is that while lesbian and gay people did not create the structure of monosexism, they were brought up in it and continue to uphold it. I personally have often found that LGBTQIA+ spaces are dominated by cis white allo gay men who tend to be uninformed about identities outside their own. And that is the issue at hand. Lesbian and gay people have been taught that m-spec identities are not valid and instead of doing the work to unlearn this, they continue to perpetuate it. The LGBTQIA+ community is a product of society as a whole and therefore has many of the same issues.

If these issues exist in society as a whole, why then such a focus on their existence in the LGBTQIA+ community? Well first, I would argue that the book thus far discusses the wider societal issue in detail. But second, and more importantly, it is due to its impact. We saw earlier that while there is more bigotry existing in wider society, the impact on m-spec people compared to the bigotry from within the LGBTQIA+ community was seen to be largely the same.

Why? Well, consider the experience of m-spec people compared to lesbian and gay people. When lesbian and gay people come out, they may face rejection from society, bigotry from their family and friends, hardship due to their identity. They may find their way to the LGBTQIA+ community, a place populated with people like them, people who have had similar experiences, people who can support them.

But for m-spec people, they may not get that support. When they enter the LGBTQIA+ community, they may find that it's mostly populated with lesbian and gay people. They may find that these people hold the same views and opinions as the general populace. M-spec people may continue to face rejection, bigotry and hardship.

Think about the barriers this creates. Instead of getting support, being able to build a network, access resources and find validity in their identity, m-spec people are erased and degraded once more. This can be a painful experience; it can be isolating. As Shearing says in their essay 'What it's like to be out but not out-out as a bisexual', 'If you can't exist safely within hetronormative society, as bisexuals can't, the thought that you can't come in from the cold into queer spaces is terrifying' (Shearing 2017).

This is what is called double discrimination– it's discrimination from both the straight community and the gay community. This is the lived experience for many m-spec people. And this plays a fundamental part in the wellbeing of m-spec people. If they are rejected from the community, they won't access these spaces. And statistics show that many m-spec people are not present in the community. This results in vital support and resources not reaching m-spec people.

Are m-spec people aware of the support groups that exist in the LGBTQIA+ community? Does vital messaging around how to conduct safer sex reach them? Do m-spec people have a community of friends, people who have shared experiences, around them?

Of course, m-spec people do not receive more bigotry from within the LGBTQIA+ community than they do outside it. The structural monosexism created by society at large, by those in power, by the heterosexual community, is what creates the barriers that m-spec people face – the poor education, the rejection and invalidation, the barriers to accessing support and so on. If I haven't made that abundantly clear as of yet, let me do so now.

The experiences of m-spec people within the LGBTQIA+ community are an extension of this structure. And it would be remiss of me not to highlight the impact it has. It creates new barriers – barriers that lesbian and gay people may not necessarily face – and leads to the worsened wellbeing of m-spec people as a result.

The m-spec community

The issue of double discrimination has prompted numerous m-spec activists to do two things. First, they have worked and continue to work within the LGBTQIA+ community to create a more inclusive environment and push the community to do better by m-spec people. We can see this in the way the community is now called the LGBTQIA+ community rather than just 'lesbian and gay', and it goes way beyond this. Our m-spec elders fought the bans, fought the bigotry and fought the lack of inclusion.

Second, they created their own spaces. Today, there are numerous m-spec groups, events and networks all over the world. In the UK, you have prominent groups like The Bisexual Index, Bi Pride UK and Biscuit, local groups like London Bisexual Meetup and Scottish Bi+ Network, events like BiCon and London BiFest, and support networks like Bi Survivors Network. In the US, you have groups like NY Area Bisexual Network, Still Bisexual, Bisexual Resource Center and countless others.

And there are so many more groups, events and communities all around the world: Bi Collective Delhi in India, Toronto Bi+ Network in Canada along with the Bi+ Arts Festival, Bi Sides in Brazil, Biszkopty in Poland, Bitopya in Turkey, visiBle Norway in Norway, Side B Philippines in the Philippines, Bi+ Collective Australia which is a group of various communities in Australia, EuroBiCon based in Europe and so so many more.

There are countless groups who provided vital resources both historically and in recent years, such as the San Francisco

Bisexual Community Center, Bis of Colour and London Bi Pandas, who unfortunately are no longer around for various reasons. Others, such as BiNet USA, have provided so much to the community but have recently fallen into disrepute. Our community has made its own spaces, created its own language, formed its own movements and even created its own flags. We have made support networks, hosted discussions, held safe spaces and even had our own parties.

The m-spec community has spent countless time, energy and money in filling the gap created by our society and left unfilled by the mainstream LGBTQIA+ community. But this hasn't been easy.

M-spec community struggles

As mentioned earlier, we saw that in the US, bi-specific organizations were getting no funding. This is despite the fact that nearly $100 million was given to LGBT causes (Andre 2012). Why is this the case? Well there are several problems here, and recent research in the UK has neatly outlined them all.

The Bi Funding Research Report (Baxter-Williams, G and Moore 2021), commissioned by the LGBT+ Consortium in 2021 and conducted by multiple bi community organizers, investigated the struggles that bi organizations face around resourcing, funding and outreach. The research revealed that the vast majority of the bi community organizers that were contacted didn't apply for funding. Why?

The majority of the bi organizations were run entirely by unpaid volunteers in their spare time. This meant that they often didn't have the time or the energy to do all the necessary administration to obtain funding – not just the form filling to apply for the grants but everything else around it. From setting up a bank account, to finding grants they were eligible for, to all the reporting and accounting, it ended up being more trouble than it was worth.

And there was no guarantee that they would be successful. The few that did endeavour to obtain funding found that they were unsuccessful and often received little to no feedback as to why. The majority agreed that applying for funding as a small, grassroots organization was pointless. They often expected not to get the money, and it is understandable why. In a monosexist society, can it really be expected that a small, grassroots m-spec organization will be prioritized for funding over other causes?

Another issue noted by bi organizations was the fact that funders assumed that by donating to LGBTQIA+ organizations, bi people were already covered. However, this often wasn't the case. We have already discussed at length the issues that bi and m-spec people face within the LGBTQIA+ community, how the bigotry and erasure often continue and how this isn't an individual issue but is systemic.

It then stands to reason that a not insignificant number of LGBTQIA+ organizations did not use their money to specifically support bi people in the community. A number of people who contributed their experiences for this report discussed how LGBTQIA+ organizations and networks often had no discussion of bi specific issues on their website and zero bi-specific support services.

The report also mentioned how these organizations often used bi trauma in order to access funding. They took statistics that combined the lesbian and gay with the bisexual to showcase how we have, for example, worse mental health, without showing the disparities between these different groups. As we have already mentioned in the health chapter, bi and m-spec people are more likely to have worse mental health than lesbian and gay people. Our issues are used in order to bolster the statistics, but the funds are then used primarily for lesbian and gay projects. This was something we also noted in the sexual health section: the idea of 'exclusion by inclusion'.

The lack of support from LGBTQIA+ organizations isn't always intentional, the report notes, but shows a lack of awareness of the issues bi people face and, more specifically, how to reach them. We have already mentioned that bi and m-spec people don't come out and are not present in LGBTQIA+ spaces. Therefore, if these organizations' programmes and projects target those in LGBTQIA+ spaces, then m-spec people are going to be missed.

What this all amounts to is that the needs of bi and m-spec people are left to bi and m-spec organizations and groups, which are very grassroots, entirely volunteer run with little or no funding. These groups are run on a shoestring budget and those involved in the organizing often result in using their own money in order to fund their work. External funding often comes from within the community, either from other m-spec organizations or from members of the community.

These organizations do an incredible job in finding ways to undertake their work and support the community in whatever way they can, with the resources they have available. But naturally this all means that they are unable to reach people, signpost to their group and support the community on a grand scale. The result is that m-spec people fall by the wayside, unable to get support. Organizing in this way also takes its toll on those in charge, who regularly experience burnout, meaning their health is impacted further.

It is clear that things need to change and this report outlines numerous recommendations, from allocating a fair share of funds to providing resources, support and training. The work these m-spec organizations are doing is incredibly important and there's more work to be done.

Pride in London

In 2017, it was reported that Pride in London, one of the biggest, if not the biggest, Pride organizations in the UK, would not have any bisexual groups marching at its event (Reid-Smith 2017). This was, according to Pride in London, due to the fact that no bi groups had applied before the deadline. After a huge uproar from the bi community, Pride in London decided to allow Bi Pride to march at the front of the UK Prides section of the parade. Bi Pride worked with other bi groups to ensure that people were involved in the march.

This was a troubling event that brought up a lot of questions. How could you have an LGBTQIA+ Pride event without any representation from the m-spec community? How could Pride in London be content, at least initially, with no m-spec groups marching in its event? Why did it not question why it hadn't seen any groups apply? Why did it not see it fit to reach out to the m-spec community and ask whether anyone was applying, or see if there were any barriers for them and try to fix that? Or did it not have any connection with the m-spec community? It should not have come to the community persistently trying to contact them for Pride in London to finally rectify the issue.

Shearing (2018) wrote about this event in an article for The Queerness, stating that Libby Baxter-Williams, director of Biscuit, kept asking Pride in London for answers as to how it could have an event without any bi+ representation and, in response, the organization called her 'demanding'. Shearing also states that it was only after a lot of yelling from prominent bi voices that 'another group gave up some of their wrist bands so the bi community could be represented'. This is a shocking state of affairs that shows an unwillingness from Pride in London to ensure proper representation.

As Shearing says, this wasn't good enough, and prompted Libby Baxter-Williams to launch a campaign for a float for the following year's Pride in London. Numerous bi+ activists were involved in the project, including Lo Shearing themselves and Marcus Morgan, founder and chair of The Bisexual Index (Mathers 2018). The project was an important but difficult undertaking. As Libby says in an article for *Gay Star News*, there were numerous 'unexpected expenses' and 'more bureaucracy than we planned for' (Mathers 2018). Libby also says how the m-spec 'community lives largely on the poverty line, so we just can't afford to do things like this regularly' (Mathers 2018).

I spoke to Lo Shearing, who was involved in this project. She told me that the whole affair cost them around £4000 and while to some groups this wouldn't be a huge expense, it was a massive hit to them. Shearing said that this money could have helped run their community, Bi Survivors Network, or Biscuit, for an entire year.

This highlights the difficult situation m-spec activists face. Due to how underfunded the m-spec community is, m-spec activists are often unable to partake in events such as Pride. Doing so means spending huge sums of money which could be used to keep their community afloat. But without being present at such events, they are unable to do the important outreach work to make their community visible to those who need it.

M-spec activism

I spoke to a few m-spec activists who have created or run communities in the UK that specifically target the m-spec community about their experiences of working within the LGBTQIA+ community.

Marcus Morgan, founder of The Bisexual Index, told me that other activists in the LGBTQIA+ community tend to be supportive but surprised, patronizingly so, to meet a bi or m-spec activist. They said that LGBTQIA+ people who aren't activists tend to be less supportive. They found that those in the LGBTQIA+ community often doubt that m-spec people face distinct issues from gay people and have a disbelief in m-spec identities in general. This is one of the important parts of the outreach work that Marcus does, being a public speaker and having people meet an m-spec person who is out and proud, giving people the space to ask questions without seeming ignorant or foolish.

John G, who runs London Bisexuals Meetup Group, told me that he is picky about the organizations he works with as he often finds himself ignored or doesn't hear back from particular groups. He often puts more trust and therefore effort into working with organizations who reach out to him first and has found plenty of inclusive organizations, but also some who say that they're inclusive but aren't. He doesn't tend to hear m-spec phobia from these groups, just empty promises, which he said could potentially be due to them being busy.

John G said that he lost a venue some years ago for their meetup when the venue got new ownership. He suspected m-spec phobia but it could have just been money grabbing, as they wanted a £1500 minimum bar take for their 50–60-person group.

Libby Baxter-Williams, who is the director at Biscuit, told me that when she first started doing stuff in the m-spec community, it was well known that Stonewall was specifically anti-m-spec and anti-trans and where Stonewall goes, others follow. She said that in 2016, Ruth Hunt (the then CEO of Stonewall) decided that the B (bisexual) and T (trans) should be part of Stonewall's remit. Hunt ran a day where she consulted with the m-spec community about what they wanted, but the results were mixed. Stonewall started explicitly including m-spec identities in their stuff, which helped build trust, but a promised report never came.

Libby said that being part of the acronym has definitely helped, as it has created a conversation around how m-spec people have been marginalized within the LGBTQIA+ community. Conversations on social media, such as Tumblr, started including m-spec identities and this knowledge has started seeping upwards in the community, helping to educate the big-name activists within the community. The culture is shifting, according to Libby, but m-spec activists often lack the connections to reach out to, and don't have the funds to go to, the events where they would make such connections, which results in the community still being inaccessible for m-spec activists.

LGBTQIA+ media organizations are often unhelpful, Libby said, as they don't tend to be interested in the m-spec community unless something scandalous has happened in our community. She noted that while m-spec celebrities get covered, m-spec issues don't. This is a trend I have noticed too, where the current issues that are impacting m-spec people are often not covered and, alongside this, the campaigns, events and other positive movements in the m-spec community aren't shown either. Libby said that, overall, working with the community can be hard and the m-spec phobia isn't entirely gone. While some LGBTQIA+ communities are more inclusive of m-spec people, it doesn't feel as if m-spec people have a seat at the table quite yet.

Lo Shearing, founder of Bi Survivors Network, told me that the large, established LGBTQIA+ groups often aren't supportive of the m-spec community. They have often seen campaigns or events that Bi Survivors Network would have been perfect for but no one has reached out to them. She says that this is likely because they're smaller but they don't have the resources to do the necessary outreach work.

Lo told me how she and Libby were considering a stall for Pride in London in 2020, but it would have cost them £200 just for the stall. She said that the m-spec community could do a lot with the £200, but without getting that stall there may be no m-spec stall at Pride and they would be unable to do the important outreach work and provide invaluable resources to m-spec people at Pride.

She said that the m-spec community is often fighting erasure and m-spec phobia not just from outside but from within the LGBTQIA+ community, where the big organizations often don't understand the value of m-spec groups as they don't recognize that m-spec people have their own, specific issues. As a result, Lo said that it often feels as if the m-spec community is having to do everything themselves, from the ground up, and is constantly playing catch-up. This is likely to be one of the reasons why m-spec activists burn out and so many groups close. This then makes things even harder as the torch is not passed down through generations, and instead everything must be rebuilt from scratch again and again.

This highlights the issues we have already mentioned: how lack of time, energy and money creates barriers for the m-spec community to be involved in events such as Pride; how the LGBTQIA+ community often isn't supportive enough of the m-spec community; and how this only furthers the issues m-spec people face in regard to feeling represented, welcome and seen within the LGBTQIA+ community. It is a vicious cycle that continually perpetuates itself.

Finding pride

With everything I have discussed in this book, finding pride in your identity sounds like an insurmountable task. With the structures of monosexism, heteronormativity, phallocentrism, and more, at play, leading to the erasure and bigotry that m-spec people face, it is no wonder that m-spec people struggle with coming out and feeling secure in their identity. It impacts every part of your life, from family life and friendships to dating and relationships, and not only does it impact your mental health but it creates further barriers for accessing mental health services, as well as sexual health services. For those who hold other marginalized identities, the issues only get worse and new ones arise.

However, through all of this, numerous m-spec men have managed to find pride in their identity. You've met many in this book. The road to accepting your identity may be difficult, but it is possible. The m-spec community can have a huge impact here. John G told me that through spending time in the m-spec community, he was able to normalize his feelings and experiences. This allowed his confidence to grow, helped him to accept his identity and inhabit LGBTQIA+ spaces as his whole self.

Of course, finding spaces isn't always easy. As mentioned previously, I used social media heavily when I first came out to find and interact with other m-spec people. Online spaces can be such a minefield, but it allows you to talk to people that otherwise might be out of reach, and connect with a community that otherwise might be inaccessible.

M-spec erasure and phobia are ever-present issues, Polis told me, and never stop hurting. So, it is important to focus your energy towards those who truly see and accept you. Polis said that he focuses on the fact that the people he loves have supported him from the start. Of course, not everyone is as fortunate. For me, I have had difficulties with people who have definitely not been fully supportive of my identity. And this, naturally, may make you want to hide your identity. It may make you regret ever being so open. This is all very understandable. But there is so much power in being open about your identity. Joseph told me that there will always be some person, some force, some organization, something that will make you feel lesser than because of the structures that be. But, he said, that after he spent a lifetime hiding his identity, he is now defiantly himself.

So, if it is safe for you to do so, I recommend grabbing these m-spec labels by the horns and making them part of your identity. Talk about it. Connect with people over it. Wave that flag loud and proud. Pushing yourself to claim that identity and being unashamed about it will give you the power to find pride in it, in your feelings and experiences.

There will always be someone to tell you no, to shut you down and rubbish your identity. You may find that those who you once held dear refuse to respect your identity. You may lose friends, family and connections over it. It can be an incredibly painful experience, but those who truly love you will support you every step of the way. And those who don't, in my opinion, are not worth keeping.

Epilogue

And with that, I bring this book to a close. There are plenty of topics I have explored throughout this book, but many others that have had only a passing mention or, in fact, haven't been included at all. Unfortunately, I could not include everything. I mean, I could, but I would still be writing this book to this day and I would definitely have run out of steam.

However, this book was never meant to be the last word on this topic. This isn't the be all and end all of the conversation. My hope is that this book can become a catalyst, a stepping stone, an object with which to further the conversation and have the salient points be discussed at length. I hope that we get even more books on the experiences of m-spec men, so that we can discuss further the wellbeing of m-spec men and we can dive further into the lives of people living with intersectional identities.

To every non-m-spec person reading this book, I hope you are now informed about the struggles that m-spec men face, the structures that birth the bigotry that plagues our lives and the impact that this has. I hope it pushes you to work with m-spec people to break down the structural barriers we contend with. To those non-m-spec people who are part of the LGBTQIA+ community, I hope you are now aware that the issues exist even within our community. I hope it inspires you to root out the bigotry within our community and make these places truly safe for us to exist in.

To every m-spec man reading this book, I hope the conversations have helped you realize that you are not alone in your journey. I hope it enables you to find the community and connect with other m-spec people, and inspires you to talk about your story. To every person reading this who may be questioning their identity, I hope this book has brought awareness of the structures at play, and how they may have been internalized, and allows you to break free of these shackles and embrace your identity. I wish each and every one of you the best on your journey.

If this books helps even one person, I will consider it a success. Here's hoping it helps you.

Acknowledgements

There are some people without whose help I would not have been able to write this book. I would like to take a moment to thank them.

Special thanks to Bren Frederick (she/her), a bisexual history scholar, activist and founder of the Bi Pan Library, for providing an invaluable number of resources and endlessly assisting me with my research. The Bi Pan Library is a physical and digital archive of bi, pan and m-spec media and history, offering research assistance and resource curation to the queer community, students, educators, journalists, organizations and anyone else curious about queer history.

Special thanks to Eloise Monteiro (she/they), volunteer for Sydney Bi+ Network, who helped me greatly in research around the barriers m-spec men face in regard to their sexual health. Sydney Bi+ Network is a volunteer-run organization dedicated to improving the wellbeing of bi+ folks in Sydney through community building, education and advocacy.

Special thanks to the m-spec activists who spoke to me about their activism for my Pride chapter:

Marcus Morgan (they/them), founder of The Bisexual Index, one of the largest groups in the UK that provides support and resources for UK bisexual activists.

Libby Baxter-Williams (she/her), director of Biscuit, a UK organization that organizes and advocates fighting biphobia with a specific focus on the intersection of biphobia and misogyny.

John G (he/him), founder of London Bisexuals Meetup Group, a social meetup group in London.

Lo Shearing (they/she), founder of Bi Survivors Network, a support and advocacy network for bi+ survivors of domestic/ sexual violence, and author of Bi the Way.

And an extra special thank you to Lo for always being available to listen to my book woes and for reviewing pieces of my writing.

Special thanks to others who helped provide me with resources, articles and works and supported my research.

Special thanks to my friends who have continually championed me and my writing, especially Can, Jack and Lee, but so many others besides. You know who you are and I love you all.

Special thanks to my boyfriend, Elliot, for being my rock during this process and picking up the slack around the flat, giving me time and space to work. I love you so much.

Special thanks to Maz Hedgehog (they/them) for conducting a fantastic sensitivity read. Maz is a writer and performer, fond of poetry and theatre, folklore and fairies, and the rule of three. Outside the arts, Maz dabbles in knitting, baking and excessive swearing. Find them on Twitter and Instagram @MazHedgehog.

Special thanks to Andrew James (he/him) and everyone at Jessica Kingsley Publishers for giving me a voice, making this book happen.

Special thanks to each and every m-spec activist who has

helped guide the way. From those who I have referenced in the book, to those who contributed. From those above who assisted with my research to many more besides, I stand on your shoulders, thank you for all your work.

And lastly, but certainly not least, a huge extra special thank you to every single person who has contributed to this book. I cannot thank these people enough for sharing their stories with me. Without you, there would be no book. The next section names each and every person who gave up their time to tell me their story.

Contributors

Alan (they/he)
Alex (he/him)
Alexander (he/they)
Ant (he/they)
Ben (he/him)
Blizzb3ar (he/him)
Bobby (he/him)
Cee (they/he)
CJ (he/him)
CJ Connor (he/they)
Drew (they/them)
Gordon (he/him)
Hann (he/they)
Ismail (he/him)
J (he/him)
Jacob (he/him)
James (he/him)
James P (he/him)

Jameson (he/they)
Jay (he/him)
John (he/him)
John B (he/him)
John G (he/him)
Joseph (he/him)
Jupiter (they/he)
K (he/him)
Kamal (he/him)
Khafre (he/him)
Levi (he/him)
Liam (he/him)
Matt (he/him)
Mikey (he/fae)
Oliver (he/him)
Osh (he/him)
Phillip (he/they)
Polis (he/him)

Quinn (they/she)
R (he/him)
Rob (he/him)
Roe (any pronouns)
Seth (he/they)
Shae (he/they)
Steve (he/him)
T (he/him)
Terence (he/him)

Terrence (he/him)
Thom (they/them)
Todd (he/him)
VR (he/him)
Will (he/him)
Xy (any pronouns, prefer they)
Y (he/him)
Zachary (he/him)

References

Representation and education

Brydum, S. (2019). *Bisexual Men Aren't 'Spreading HIV'*. [Online]. Accessed on 02/05/21 at www.hivplusmag.com/stigma/2019/9/19/bisexual-men-arent-spreading-hiv.

Campanile, C. (2014). *Women with Bisexual Partners Account for New HIV Cases: Study*. [Online]. Accessed on 02/05/21 at https://nypost.com/2014/01/01/women-with-bisexual-partners-account-for-new-hiv-cases-study.

GLAAD. *Where We Are On TV. Report: 2009–2010 Season*. [Online]. Accessed on 02/05/21 at www.glaad.org/sites/default/files/whereweareontv2009-2010.pdf.

GLAAD. *Where We Are On TV. Report 2014*. [Online]. Accessed on 02/05/21 at www.glaad.org/files/GLAAD-2014-WWAT.pdf.

GLAAD. *Where We Are On TV. Report 2019*. [Online]. Accessed on 02/05/21 at www.glaad.org/sites/default/files/GLAAD%20WHERE%20WE%20ARE%20ON%20TV%202019%202020.pdf.

Griffiths, G. (2020). *Buffy The Vampire Slayer Creator Would Make Willow Bisexual in Modern-Day Remake After Being Persuaded Against*

It: 'We're not ready for that'. [Online]. Accessed on 02/05/21 at https://metro.co.uk/2020/05/19/joss-whedon-admits-willow-bisexual-buffy-vampire-slayer-remake-12727558.

Kuhr, E. (2020). High Schools Must Teach LGBTQ-inclusive Sex Education in England. [Online]. Accessed on 02/05/21 at www.nbcnews.com/feature/nbc-out/high-schools-must-teach-lgbtq-inclusive-sex-education-england-n1239514.

LGBT Fans Deserve Better. (n.d.). Trope: Just an Experiment. [Online]. Accessed on 02/05/21 at https://web.archive.org/web/20210209061653/https://lgbtfansdeservebetter.com/tropes/just-an-experiment.

LGBT HealthLink. (n.d.). The Bisexual History of HIV/AIDS, in Photos. [Online]. Accessed on 02/05/21 at https://blog.lgbthealthlink.org/2015/01/29/the-bisexual-history-of-hivaids-in-photos.

LGBT History Month. (n.d.). Section 28. [Online]. Accessed on 02/05/21 at https://lgbtplushistorymonth.co.uk/wp-content/uploads/2020/02/1384014531S28Background.pdf.

Malebranche, D.J., Arriola, K.J., Jenkins, T.R., Dauria, E. & Patel, S.N. (2010). 'Exploring the "Bisexual Bridge": A qualitative study of risk behavior and disclosure of same-sex behavior among Black bisexual men.' American Journal of Public Health, 100(1), 159–164.

Movement Advancement Project. (2016). Invisible Majority: The Disparities Facing Bisexual People and How to Remedy Them. [Online]. Accessed on 23/01/22 at www.lgbtmap.org/file/invisible-majority.pdf.

Nordheimer, J. (1987). AIDS Specter for Women: The Bisexual Man. [Online]. Accessed on 02/05/21 at www.nytimes.com/1987/04/03/us/aids-specter-for-women-the-bisexual-man.html.

Planned Parenthood. (2015). Lack of Comprehensive Sex Education Puts LGBTQ Youth at Risk: National Organizations Issue Call to Action to Improve Programs and Policies. [Online]. Accessed on 25/01/22 at www.plannedparenthood.org/about-us/newsroom/

press-releases/lack-of-comprehensive-sex-education-puts-
lgbtq-youth-at-risk-national-organizations-issue-call-to-
action-to-improve-programs-and.

Public Religion Research Institute. (2015). *How Race and Religion
Shape Millennial Attitudes on Sexuality and Reproductive Health.*
[Online]. Accessed on 02/05/21 at www.prri.org/wp-content/
uploads/2015/03/PRRI-Millennials-Web-FINAL.pdf.

Schwartz, S. (2019). *Four States Now Require Schools to Teach LGBT
History.* [Online]. www.edweek.org/teaching-learning/four-
states-now-require-schools-to-teach-lgbt-history/2019/08.

Shearing, L. (2019). *Introducing the Ramirez Test.* [Online]. Accessed
on 02/05/21 at https://medium.com/@lois.shearing/introducing-
the-ramirez-test-b91e98b57d1d.

SIECUS. (2020). *Lack of State Sex Ed Regulation Puts Students in Danger
of Receiving Harmful Lessons, Report Finds.* [Online]. Accessed on
02/05/21 at https://siecus.org/state-profiles-2019-announcement.

Stonewall. (2017). *School Report – The Experiences of Lesbian, Gay, Bi
and Trans Pupils in Britain's Schools in 2017.* [Online]. Accessed
on 25/01/22 at www.stonewall.org.uk/system/files/the_school_
report_2017.pdf.

Stonewall. (2019). *LGBT-inclusive Education: Everything You Need to
Know.* [Online]. Accessed on 02/05/21 at www.stonewall.org.uk/
lgbt-inclusive-education-everything-you-need-know.

Thames TV. (2016). *David Bowie/Interview/Afternoon Plus/1979.*
[Online]. YouTube. Accessed on 11/5/21 at www.youtube.com/
watch?v=LwTFW4kfHl4&t=347s.

TV Tropes. *Ambiguously Bi.* [Online]. Accessed on 02/05/21 at https://
tvtropes.org/pmwiki/pmwiki.php/Main/AmbiguouslyBi.

TV Tropes. *Anything That Moves.* [Online]. Accessed on 02/05/21
at https://tvtropes.org/pmwiki/pmwiki.php/Main/Anything
ThatMoves.

TV Tropes. *Depraved Bisexual.* [Online]. Accessed on 02/05/21 at https://tvtropes.org/pmwiki/pmwiki.php/Main/Depraved Bisexual.

TV Tropes. *No Bisexuals.* [Online]. Accessed on 02/05/21 at https://tvtropes.org/pmwiki/pmwiki.php/Main/NoBisexuals.

Two Bi Guys. (2021). *Shiri Eisner on Re-imagining Bisexual Masculinity.* [Online]. Accessed on 02/05/21 at https://creator.zencastr.com/z/nNuaZ--Y.

Wright, M. (2019). *Freddie Mercury: What REALLY Happened with Mary Austin When He Came Out – in Her Words.* [Online]. Accessed on 02/05/21 at www.express.co.uk/entertainment/music/1214023/Freddie-Mercury-Queen-Mary-Austin-relationship-gay-girl friend.

Coming out

Andre, A., Brown, J., Delpercio, A., Kahn, E., Nicoll, A. & Sherouse, B. (2014). *Supporting and Caring for Our Bisexual Youth.* Washington DC: The Human Rights Campaign Foundation. [Online]. The Human Rights Campaign. Accessed on 02/05/21 at https://assets2.hrc.org/files/assets/resources/Supporting_and_Caring_for_Bisexual_Youth.pdf.

Chibbarro Jr., L. (2019). *FBI Report Shows Increase in Anti-LGBT hate crimes.* [Online]. Washington Blade. Accessed on 02/05/21 at www.washingtonblade.com/2019/11/20/fbi-report-shows-increase-in-anti-lgbt-hate-crimes.

Desmond, E. & Nickodemus, L. (eds). (2017). *The Bi-ble: An Anthology of Personal Narratives and Essays About Bisexuality.* Edinburgh: Monstrous Regiment Publishing.

Desmond, E. & Nickodemus, L. (eds). (2019). *The Bi-ble: New Testimonials.* Edinburgh: Monstrous Regiment Publishing.

Eisner, S. (2013). *The Difference Between Monosexism and Biphobia.*

[Online]. Bi Radical. Accessed on 02/05/21 at https://radicalbi. wordpress.com/2013/02/08/the-difference-between-mono sexism-and-biphobia.

Francis, S. (2020). *Call for law change over increase in homophobic hate crimes in London.* [Online]. BBC News. Accessed on 02/05/21 at www.bbc.co.uk/news/uk-england-london-51049336.

Kate, M.E. & Deaux, K. (1987). 'Gender belief systems: Homosexuality and the implicit inversion theory.' *Psychology of Women Quarterly,* 11(1), 83–96.

LGBT History Month. (n.d.). *Section 28.* [Online]. Accessed on 02/05/21 at https://lgbtplushistorymonth.co.uk/wp-content/ uploads/2020/02/1384014531S28Background.pdf.

McCreary, D.R. (1994). 'The male role and avoiding femininity.' *Sex Roles,* 31(9), 517–531.

Milton, J. (2021). *Gay and Bisexual Men Earn Thousands Less Than Their Straight Peers, Eye-Opening Study Finds.* [Online]. Accessed on 25/01/22 at www.pinknews.co.uk/2021/07/30/gay-bisexual-straight-pay-gap-study.

Movement Advancement Project. (2016). *Invisible Majority: The Disparities Facing Bisexual People and How to Remedy Them.* [Online]. Accessed on 23/01/22 at www.lgbtmap.org/file/invisible-majority. pdf.

Ochs, R. & Sharif Williams, H. (eds). (2015). *Recognize: The Voices of Bisexual Men.* Boston, MA: Bisexual Resource Center.

Pew Research Center. (2013). *A Survey of LGBT Americans.* [Online]. Accessed on 02/05/21 at www.pewresearch.org/social-trends/ wp-content/uploads/sites/3/2013/06/SDT_LGBT-Americans_ 06-2013.pdf.

R., M. (2015). 'Phallocentrism and Bisexual Invisibility.' In R. Ochs & H. Sharif Williams (eds) *Recognize: The Voices of Bisexual Men.* Boston, MA: Bisexual Resource Center.

Sears, B. & Mallory, C. (2011). *Documented Evidence of Employment*

Discrimination & Its Effects on LGBT People. [Online]. The Williams Institute. Accessed on 02/05/21 at https://williamsinstitute.law.ucla.edu/wp-content/uploads/Effects-LGBT-Employ-Discrim-Jul-2011.pdf.

SIECUS. (2020). *Lack of State Sex Ed Regulation Puts Students in Danger of Receiving Harmful Lessons, Report Finds.* [Online]. SIECUS. Accessed on 02/05/21 at https://siecus.org/state-profiles-2019-announcement.

Stonewall. (2017). *School Report - The experiences of lesbian, gay, bi and trans pupils in Britain's schools in 2017.* [Online]. Accessed on 25/01/22 at www.stonewall.org.uk/system/files/the_school_report_2017.pdf.

Stonewall. (2018a). *LGBT In Britain – Home and Communities.* [Online]. Accessed on 23/01/22 at www.stonewall.org.uk/sites/default/files/lgbt_in_britain_home_and_communities.pdf.

Stonewall. (2018b). *LGBT In Britain – University Report.* [Online]. Accessed on 02/05/21 at www.stonewall.org.uk/system/files/lgbt_in_britain_universities_report.pdf.

Stonewall. (2018c). *LGBT In Britain – Work Report.* [Online]. Accessed on 02/05/21 at www.stonewall.org.uk/system/files/lgbt_in_britain_work_report.pdf.

White, D. (2016). *Match Explores Dating Habits of LGBTQ Singles in US with New Study.* [Online]. Global Dating Insights. Accessed on 02/05/21 at www.globaldatinginsights.com/news/match-explores-dating-habits-of-us-lgbtq-singles-in-new-study.

Dating and relationships

Bi Pride UK. (2021). *Bi Pride UK 2021.* [Online]. YouTube. Accessed on 23/01/22 at www.youtube.com/watch?v=4dUbAcqiDBM.

CDC. (2010). *NISVS: An Overview of 2010 Findings on Victimization by*

Sexual Orientation. [Online]. Accessed on 23/01/22 at www.cdc. gov/violenceprevention/pdf/cdc_nisvs_victimization_final-a. pdf.

Cosmopolitan. (2019). *Why These Women Prefer Sex with Bisexual Men.* [Online]. Accessed on 23/01/22 at www.cosmopolitan.com/uk/ love-sex/sex/a28536377/sex-with-bisexual-men.

Galop. (2022). *The Use of Sexual Violence as an Attempt to Convert or Punish LGBT+ People in the UK.* [Online]. Accessed on 23/01/22 at https://galop.org.uk/wp-content/uploads/2022/01/The-Use-of-Sexual-Violence-as-an-Attempt-to-Convert-or-Punish-LGBT-People-in-the-UK.pdf.

Garrido, N. (2020). *The Case of Javier Vilalta Reveals the Gap Between the Judiciary and Sexual Diversity.* [Online, Translated]. Accessed on 23/01/22 at www.elsaltodiario.com/lgtbiq/javier-vilalta-sentencia-condena-bisexualidad-revela-desfase-judicatura-diversidad-sexual-.

Haupert, M.L., Gesselman, A.N., Moors, A.C, Fisher, H.E. & Garcia, J.R. (2017). 'Prevalence of experiences with consensual nonmonogamous relationships: Findings from two national samples of single Americans.' *Journal of Sex & Marital Therapy*, 43(5), 424–440.

Hertlein, K.M., Hartwell, E.E. & Munns, M.E. (2016). 'Attitudes toward bisexuality according to sexual orientation and gender.' *GSEAP Faculty Publications*, 126.

Hope, R. (2019). *Common Misconceptions About Polyamory.* [Online]. Accessed on 29/12/20 at https://medium.com/polyamory-today/ common-misconceptions-about-polyamory-991097faaa81.

Hy, M. (2019). *What Do You Call Your Flavour of Non-monogamy?* [Online]. Accessed on 29/12/20 at https://polyamorouswhileasian. com/articles/what-do-you-call-your-flavor-of-non-monogamy.

Maurice, E.M. (2020). *Bisexual Man Ordered to Pay Ex-wife Thousands After She Accused Him of Hiding His Homosexuality. Only, He's Not Gay.* [Online]. Accessed on 23/01/22 at www.pinknews.

co.uk/2020/12/08/javier-vilalta-bisexual-man-ex-wife-lawsuit-hide-homosexuality-court-order-compensation.

Stonewall. (2020). *LGBT in Britain – Bi Report*. [Online]. Accessed on 23/01/22 at www.stonewall.org.uk/system/files/lgbt_in_britain_bi.pdf.

Yussuf, J.R. (2021). 'Bisexual Men Are the Best in Bed' Is Fetishistic Biphobia. [Online]. Accessed on 26/01/22 at https://web.archive.org/web/20210823072403/https://www.wearyourvoicemag.com/bisexual-men-fetishistic-biphobia.

Zava. (n.d.). *Sexual Journeys*. [Online]. Accessed on 29/12/20 at www.zavamed.com/uk/sexual-journeys.html.

Health

Movement Advancement Project. (2016). *Invisible Majority: The Disparities Facing Bisexual People and How to Remedy Them*. [Online]. Accessed on 23/01/22 at www.lgbtmap.org/file/invisible-majority.pdf.

Rainbow Health Ontario. (n.d.). RHO Fact Sheet: Bisexual Health. [Online]. Accessed on 23/01/22 at www.rainbowhealthontario.ca/wp-content/uploads/2011/06/RHO_FactSheet_BIHEALTH_E.pdf.

Stonewall. (2018). *LGBT in Britain – Health Report*. [Online]. Accessed on 23/01/22 at www.stonewall.org.uk/system/files/lgbt_in_britain_health.pdf.

Stonewall. (2020). *LGBT in Britain – Bi Report*. [Online]. Accessed on 23/01/22 at www.stonewall.org.uk/system/files/lgbt_in_britain_bi.pdf.

Mental health

American Psychiatry Association. (n.d.). *Stigma, Prejudice and Discrimination Against People with Mental Illness*. [Online]. Accessed on 28/11/21 at www.psychiatry.org/patients-families/stigma-and-discrimination.

Badgett, M.V.L., Durso, L.E. & Schneebaum, A. (2013). *New Patterns of Poverty in the Lesbian, Gay, and Bisexual Community*. [Online]. Accessed on 23/01/22 at https://williamsinstitute.law.ucla.edu/wp-content/uploads/Poverty-LGB-Jun-2013.pdf.

Bailey, J.M., Holmes, L., Hsu, K.J., Jabbour, J. et al. (2020). 'Robust evidence for bisexual orientation among men.' *Proceedings of the National Academy of Sciences*, 117(3), 18369–18377.

Bawden, A., Campbell, D. & Duncan, P. (2018). *Hundreds of Mental Health Patients Died After NHS Care Failures*. [Online]. Accessed on 23/01/22 at www.theguardian.com/society/2018/mar/05/hundreds-of-mental-health-patients-dying-after-nhs-care-failures.

Chatmon, B.N. (2020). 'Males and mental health stigma.' *American Journal of Men's Health*, 14(4), 1–3.

Fraga, J. (2021). *Therapy for Every Budget: How to Access It*. [Online]. Accessed on 28/11/21 at www.healthline.com/health/therapy-for-every-budget.

Gregory, A. (2019). *More Than 120,000 NHS Patients Kept on 'hidden waiting lists' for Mental Health Appointments*. [Online]. Accessed on 28/11/21 at www.independent.co.uk/news/health/nhs-mental-health-treatment-therapy-waiting-list-appointment-a9079541.html.

KFF. (n.d.). *Mental Health Care Health Professional Shortage Areas (HPSAs)*. [Online]. Last updated 30/09/21. Accessed on 23/01/22 at www.kff.org/other/state-indicator/mental-health-care-health-professional-shortage-areas-hpsas.

Leonhardt, M. (2021). *What You Need to Know About the Cost and Accessibility of Mental Health Care in America*. [Online]. Accessed on 23/01/22 at www.cnbc.com/2021/05/10/cost-and-accessibility-of-mental-health-care-in-america.html.

Mental Health Foundation. (n.d.). *Stigma and Discrimination*. [Online]. Last updated 4/10/21. Accessed on 28/11/21 at www. mentalhealth.org.uk/a-to-z/s/stigma-and-discrimination.

Page, E.H. (2004). 'Mental health services experiences of bisexual women and bisexual men.' *Journal of Bisexuality*, 4(1–2), 137–160.

Pallotta-Chiarolli, M. (2016). *Women in Relationships with Bisexual Men: Bi Men By Women*. Washington DC: Lexington Books.

Sexual health

Abif, K.K. (2019). *The Importance of Finding Support*. [Online]. Accessed on 23/01/22 at https://h-i-v.net/living/finding-support.

Avert. (n.d.). *Treatment as Prevention (TasP) for HIV*. [Online]. Accessed on 23/01/22 at www.avert.org/professionals/hiv-programming/ prevention/treatment-as-prevention.

Binson, D., Catania, J.A., Gurvey, J., Kahn, J.G. & Pollack, L.M. (1997). 'How many HIV infections cross the bisexual bridge? An estimate from the United States.' *AIDS*, 11(8), 1031–1037.

Bi Stuff. (2020). *The bisexual bench in HIV/Aids health promotion work*. [Online]. Accessed on 23/01/22 at https://bistuff.org.uk/the-bisexual-bench-in-hiv-aids-health-promotion-work.

CDC. (n.d.). *How Effective is PrEP?* [Online]. Accessed on 23/01/22 at www.cdc.gov/hiv/basics/prep/prep-effectiveness.html.

Coates, T.J., Collette, L., Ekstrand, M.L., Guydish, J.R., Hauck, W.W. & Hülle, S.B. (1994). 'Are bisexually identified men in San Francisco a common vector for spreading HIV infection to women?' *American Journal of Public Health*, 84(6), 915–919.

Crawford, J., Kippax, S. & Prestage, G. (2020). 'Not Gay, Not Bisexual, but Polymorphously Sexually Active: Male Bisexuality and AIDS in Australia.' In P. Aggleton (ed.) *Bisexualities and AIDS: International Perspectives*. London: Routledge.

Cruz, E. (2014). *STUDY: Biphobia Puts Bisexual Men at Risk for STIs*. [Online]. Accessed on 23/01/22 at www.advocate.com/

bisexuality/2014/06/26/study-biphobia-puts-bisexual-men-risk-stis.

Dodge, B. (2015). 'Scientific Research on Bisexual Men: What Do We Know, and Why Don't We Know More?' In R. Ochs & H. Sharif Williams (eds) *Recognize: The Voices of Bisexual Men.* Boston, MA: Bisexual Resource Center.

Dodge, B. & Feinstein, B.A. (2020). 'Meeting the sexual health needs of bisexual men in the age of biomedical HIV prevention: Gaps and priorities.' *Archives of Sexual Behavior,* 49(1), 217–232.

Get The Facts. (n.d). *Do Condoms Protect Against All STIs?* [Online]. Accessed on 23/01/22 at www.getthefacts.health.wa.gov.au/faqs/do-condoms-protect-against-all-stis.

HIV.gov. (n.d.). *Ready, Set, PrEP Expands Access to HIV Prevention Medications.* [Online]. Accessed on 23/01/22 at www.hiv.gov/federal-response/ending-the-hiv-epidemic/prep-program.

Holland, K. (2019). *Everything You Need to Know About Using a Dental Dam.* [Online]. Accessed on 23/01/22 at www.healthline.com/health/healthy-sex/dental-dam.

iwantprepnow. [Online]. Accessed on 23/01/22 at www.iwantprepnow.co.uk/about.

Kasadha, B. (2019). *What Does Undetectable = Untransmittable (U=U) Mean?* [Online]. Accessed on 23/01/22 at www.aidsmap.com/about-hiv/what-does-undetectable-untransmittable-uu-mean.

LGBTIQ+ Health Australia (2018). *The Cycle of Invisibility – A Model for Understanding Exclusion.* [Online]. Accessed on 23/01/22 at https://d3n8a8pro7vhmx.cloudfront.net/lgbtihealth/pages/641/attachments/original/1585266510/Cycle-of-invisibility-digital-final-PDF.pdf?1585266510.

NHS. (n.d.). *Female Condoms.* [Online]. Accessed on 23/01/22 at www.nhs.uk/conditions/contraception/female-condoms.

Pallotta-Chiarolli, M. (2016). *Women in Relationships with Bisexual Men: Bi Men By Women.* Washington DC: Lexington Books.

Planned Parenthood. (n.d.). *What is PEP?* [Online]. Accessed on 23/01/22 at www.plannedparenthood.org/learn/stds-hiv-safer-sex/hiv-aids/pep.

Prepster. (n.d.). *Vaxster! Vaccinations for Sexual Health FAQs.* [Online]. Accessed on 23/01/22 at https://prepster.info/vaxster.

Pryor, D.W., Weinberg, M.S. & Williams, C.J. (1994). *Dual Attraction: Understanding Bisexuality.* New York, NY: Oxford University Press.

Shearing, L. (2021). *Bi the Way: The Bisexual Guide to Life.* London: Jessica Kingsley Publishers.

Winderl, A.M. (2016). *These Are the STIs That Condoms Don't Protect Against.* [Online]. Accessed on 23/01/22 at www.self.com/story/these-are-the-stds-that-condoms-dont-protect-against.

Your Sexual Health. (2020). *How Often Should I Take an STD Test?* [Online]. Accessed on 23/01/22 at https://yoursexualhealth.co.uk/blog/how-often-should-i-take-an-std-test.

Intersectionality

National Association of Independent Schools. (2018). *Kimberlé Crenshaw: What is Intersectionality?* [Online]. Accessed on 28/01/22 at www.youtube.com/watch?v=ViDtnfQ9FHc.

Perlman, M. (2018). *The Origin of the Term 'intersectionality'.* [Online]. Accessed on 28/01/22 at www.cjr.org/language_corner/intersectionality.php.

Stonewall. (2018). *LGBT in Britain – Health Report.* [Online]. Accessed on 23/01/22 at www.stonewall.org.uk/system/files/lgbt_in_britain_health.pdf.

Stonewall. (2020). *LGBT in Britain – Bi Report.* [Online]. Accessed on 23/01/22 at www.stonewall.org.uk/system/files/lgbt_in_britain_bi.pdf.

Unicorn March. (n.d.). *What Do Aces Face?* [Online]. Accessed on

28/01/22 at http://web.archive.org/web/20201121045813/https://www.unicornmarch.org/Ace%20Infographic.pdf.

M-spec and trans

Abrams, M. (2020). *Gender Essentialism Is Flawed — Here's Why*. [Online]. Accessed on 23/01/22 at www.healthline.com/health/gender-essentialism.

Ainsworth, C. (2018). *Sex Redefined: The Idea of 2 Sexes is Overly Simplistic*. [Online]. Accessed on 23/01/22 at www.scientificamerican.com/article/sex-redefined-the-idea-of-2-sexes-is-overly-simplistic1.

BBC. (2019). *Transgender Hate Crimes Recorded by Police Go Up 81%*. [Online]. Accessed on 23/01/22 at www.bbc.co.uk/news/uk-48756370.

Black, R. (2021). *Stop Trying to Out-Science Transphobes*. [Online]. Accessed on 23/01/22 at https://slate.com/technology/2021/03/transphobes-science-trap-basic-human-rights.html.

Bull, R., Cunningham, N., Forstater, M. & Hilton, E. (2021). *Welcome to Sex Matters*. [Online]. Accessed on 23/01/22 at https://sex-matters.org/posts/updates/welcome-to-sex-matters.

Burns, K. (2019). *The Rise Of Anti-trans 'Radical' Feminists, Explained*. [Online]. Accessed on 23/01/22 at www.vox.com/identities/2019/9/5/20840101/terfs-radical-feminists-gender-critical.

Clements, K.C. (2021). *What Does it Mean to Be Cissexist?* [Online]. Accessed on 23/01/22 at www.healthline.com/health/transgender/cissexist.

Eisner, S. (2013). *Bi: Notes for a Bisexual Revolution*. Berkeley, CA: Seal Press.

Francis, S. (2020). *Call for Law Change Over Increase in Homophobic Hate Crimes in London*. [Online]. BBC News. Accessed on 02/05/21 at www.bbc.co.uk/news/uk-england-london-51049336.

Gardner, C.M. (2019). *A Trans Activist's Memoir is a Monumental*

Contribution to Queer History. [Online]. Accessed on 23/01/22 at https://hyperallergic.com/521846/we-both-laughed-in-pleasure-the-selected-diaries-of-lou-sullivan.

Gender Identity Clinic. (n.d.). *Waiting Times.* [Online]. Accessed on 23/01/22 at https://gic.nhs.uk/appointments/waiting-times.

Get The L Out UK. (n.d.). [Online]. Accessed on 23/01/22 at www.gettheloutuk.com/index.html.

Hilton E.M. & Wright, C.M. (2020). *The Dangerous Denial of Sex.* [Online]. Accessed on 23/01/22 at www.wsj.com/amp/articles/the-dangerous-denial-of-sex-11581638089.

Hulme, J. (2019). *Transphobes and Trans Men.* [Online]. Accessed on 22/8/22 at https://jayhulme.com/blog/transmen

Jakubowski, K. (2018). *No, the Existence of Trans People Doesn't Validate Gender Essentialism.* [Online]. Accessed on 23/01/22 at www.opendemocracy.net/en/transformation/no-existence-of-trans-people-doesn-t-validate-gender-essentialism.

Knox, L. (2019). *Media's 'Detransition' Narrative is Fueling Misconceptions, Trans Advocates Say.* [Online]. Accessed on 23/01/22 at www.nbcnews.com/feature/nbc-out/media-s-detransition-narrative-fueling-misconceptions-trans-advocates-say-n1102686.

Masson, S. (2019). *Lesbian Visibility Matters Now More Than Ever.* [Online]. Accessed on 23/01/22 at www.feministcurrent.com/2019/06/18/lesbian-visibility-matters-now-more-than-ever.

Medcalf, K. (2019). *Dispelling Myths Around Detransition.* [Online]. Accessed on 23/01/22 at www.stonewall.org.uk/about-us/news/dispelling-myths-around-detransition.

Megan Rohrer. (2010). *Lou Sullivan: Battling Gender Specialists.* [Online]. YouTube. Accessed on 23/01/21 at www.youtube.com/watch?v=SxgZNNX-v2g.

Parsons, V. (2020). *In True Boris Johnson Fashion, the 'New' Gender Clinics Announced by His Government Aren't Even New.* [Online]. Accessed on 23/01/22 at www.pinknews.co.uk/2020/09/22/

liz-truss-gender-clinic-pilot-gender-recognition-act-transgender-dysphoria.

Shearing, L. (2021). *Bi the Way: The Bisexual Guide to Life*. London: Jessica Kingsley Publishers.

Stonewall. (n.d.). *What Does the UK Government Announcement on the Gender Recognition Act Mean?* [Online]. Accessed on 23/01/22 at www.stonewall.org.uk/what-does-uk-government-announcement-gender-recognition-act-mean.

Stonewall. (2018a). *LGBT in Britain – Health Report*. [Online]. Accessed on 23/01/22 at www.stonewall.org.uk/system/files/lgbt_in_britain_health.pdf.

Stonewall. (2018b). *LGBT in Britain – Home and Communities Report*. [Online]. Accessed on 23/01/22 at www.stonewall.org.uk/sites/default/files/lgbt_in_britain_home_and_communities.pdf.

Sun, S.D. (2019). *Stop Using Phony Science to Justify Transphobia*. [Online]. Accessed on 23/01/22 at https://blogs.scientificamerican.com/voices/stop-using-phony-science-to-justify-transphobia.

M-spec and People of Colour (POC)

Applebee, J. (2015). *The Bi's of Colour History Survey Report*. [Online]. Accessed on 23/01/22 at https://bisexualresearch.files.wordpress.com/2015/06/bis-of-colour-survey-report.pdf.

Applebee, J. (2018). 'Bisexuals of Color.' In K. Harrad (ed.) *Claiming the B in LGBT: Illuminating the Bisexual Narrative*. Portland, OR: Thorntree Press.

Buckle, L. (2020). *African Sexuality and the Legacy of Imported Homophobia*. [Online]. Accessed on 23/01/22 at www.stonewall.org.uk/about-us/news/african-sexuality-and-legacy-imported-homophobia.

Cherry, K. (2021). *What is a Collectivist Culture?* [Online]. Accessed on 23/02/22 at www.verywellmind.com/what-are-collectivistic-cultures-2794962.

Stonewall (2018). *LGBT In Britain – Home and Communities Report.* [Online]. Accessed on 23/01/22 at www.stonewall.org.uk/sites/default/files/lgbt_in_britain_home_and_communities.pdf.

M-spec and A-spec

Abrams, M. (2019). *47 Terms that Describe Sexual Attraction, Behavior, and Orientation.* [Online]. Accessed on 23/01/22 at www.healthline.com/health/different-types-of-sexuality.

Arco-Pluris. (n.d.). *Monosexism × Zedsexism.* [Online]. Accessed on 23/01/22 at https://arco-pluris.tumblr.com/post/171079027942/monosexism-alosexism.

Barker, M.-J. (n.d.). *All About Amatonormativity: The Privileging of Romantic Love.* [Online]. Accessed on 23/01/22 at www.rewriting-the-rules.com/love-commitment/all-about-amatonormativity-the-privileging-of-romantic-love.

Brake, E. (n.d.). *Amatonormativity.* [Online]. Accessed on 23/01/22 at https://elizabethbrake.com/amatonormativity.

Eisner, S. (2013). *The Difference Between Monosexism and Biphobia.* [Online]. Bi Radical. Accessed on 02/05/21 at https://radicalbi.wordpress.com/2013/02/08/the-difference-between-monosexism-and-biphobia.

Ferguson, S. (2019). *What Does It Mean to Be Allosexual?* [Online]. Accessed on 23/01/22 at www.healthline.com/health/allosexual.

OULGBTQ+ Society. (n.d.). *Ace/Aro Mythbusting.* [Online]. Accessed on 23/01/22 at www.oulgbtq.org/acearo-mythbusting.html.

The Asexual Visibility & Education Network. (n.d.). *Overview.* [Online]. Accessed on 23/01/22 at www.asexuality.org/?q=overview.html.

Western Aces. (n.d.). *Terminology.* [Online]. Accessed on 23/01/22 at https://wp.wwu.edu/westernaces/terminology.

The importance of intersectionality

King, J. (2021). *Fat Trans People Are Having Their Lives Put on Hold*

Because of Devastating Medical Fatphobia. [Online]. Accessed on 28/01/22 at www.pinknews.co.uk/2021/11/19/fat-trans-medical-fatphobia.

Knights, K. (n.d.). *Disabled, Autistic, Queer ... in-between Closets – LGBTQ+ History Month.* [Online]. Accessed on 28/01/22 at https://nono-cocoa.com/blogs/news/disabled-autistic-queer-in-between-closets-lgbtq-history-month.

Thee, L. (2021). *A Tale of Two Spectrums: The Challenges of Being Both Queer and Autistic.* [Online]. Accessed on 28/01/22 at https://shamelessmag.com/blog/entry/a-tale-of-two-spectrums-the-challenges-of-being-both-queer-and-autistic.

Pride

Andre, A. (2012). *Show Us the Money: Funding for Bisexual Community Lacking.* [Online]. Accessed on 23/01/22 at www.huffpost.com/entry/bisexual-funding_b_1178932.

Baxter-Williams, L., G, J. & Moore, J. (2021). *Bi Funding Research Report.* [Online]. Accessed on 23/01/22 at www.consortium.lgbt/wp-content/uploads/2019/07/BiFundingResearchReportFullLength20210815.pdf.

Bi History. (2018). Instagram Post. [Online]. Accessed on 23/01/22 at www.instagram.com/p/BihQok6joFA.

Bi-Monthly. (1985). 'London Lesbian and Gay Centre: Bisexuals still banned.' *Bi-Monthly*, 9, 3. Retrieved from the Hall-Carpenter Archives collection at LSE Library.

Global Resources Report. 2017/2018. Government and Philanthropic Support for Lesbian, Gay, Bisexual, Transgender, and Intersex Communities. (2020) [Online]. Accessed on 23/01/22 at https://globalresourcesreport.org/wp-content/uploads/2020/05/GRR_2017-2018_Color.pdf.

Greenesmith, H. (2018). *We Know Biphobia Is Harmful. But Do We Know What's Behind It?* [Online]. Accessed on 23/01/22 at https://rewirenewsgroup.com/article/2018/04/25/know-biphobia-harmful-know-whats-behind.

Mathers, C. (2018). *This Float Was Pride In London's First Bi Community Float in 46 years.* [Online]. Accessed on 23/01/22 at www.gaystarnews.com/article/float-bisexual-pride-london.

Reid-Smith, T. (2017). *Pride in London Will Allow Bisexual Groups to March After Rescue Deal.* [Online]. Accessed on 23/01/22 at www.gaystarnews.com/article/pride-london-will-allow-bisexual-groups-march-rescue-deal.

Rust, P.C. (1995). *Bisexuality and the Challenge to Lesbian Politics: Sex, Loyalty, and Revolution.* New York, NY: NYU Press.

Shearing, L. (2017). *What It's Like to Be Out but Not Out-Out as a Bisexual.* [Online]. Accessed on 23/01/22 at https://thequeerness.com/2017/11/02/what-its-like-to-be-out-but-not-out-out-as-a-bisexual.

Shearing, L. (2018). *Why London Pride's First Bi Float Was So Important.* [Online]. Accessed on 23/01/22 at https://thequeerness.com/2018/08/01/why-london-prides-first-bi-float-was-so-important/

Shearing, L. (2021). *Bi the Way: The Bisexual Guide to Life.* London: Jessica Kingsley Publishers.

Smith, D. (1985). 'Banned: Bisexual Groups Banned from the Lesbian and Gay Centre.' *Bi-Monthly*, 8, 2–3. Retrieved from the Hall-Carpenter Archives collection at LSE Library.

Stone, S.D. (1996). 'Bisexual women and the "threat" to lesbian space: Or what if all the lesbians leave?' *Frontiers: A Journal of Women Studies*, 16(1), 101–116.

Stonewall. (2018). *LGBT in Britain – Home and Communities Report.* [Online]. Accessed on 23/01/22 at www.stonewall.org.uk/sites/default/files/lgbt_in_britain_home_and_communities.pdf.

Index